THE
STRANGEST
RUGBY
QUIZ
BOOK

First published in the United Kingdom in 2019 by
Portico
Pavilion Books Group Limited
43 Great Ormond Street
London
WC1N 3HZ

An imprint of Pavilion Books Company Ltd

ISBN 978-1-91162-221-5

A CIP catalogue record for this book is available from the British Library.

10 9 8 7 6 5 4 3 2 1

Reproduction by Mission Productions Ltd, Hong Kong
Printed and bound by Imak Offset, Turkey

This book can be ordered direct from the publisher at www.pavilionbooks.com

THE
STRANGEST®
RUGBY
QUIZ
BOOK

PORTICO

CONTENTS

INTRODUCTION

Quizzing is enjoying a golden age. Never
before has British television – or radio
for that matter – offered such a wealth
of general knowledge quizzes to enjoy.
Programmes range from the daily tea-time
game shows to the daddy and most serious
of them all, *University Challenge*, which is
still going strong more than 55 years since
its first airing. These programmes might
be billed as light entertainment for viewers
or listeners, but it is a serious business to
those taking part, with some even prepared
to exercise their general knowledge in
pursuit of prize money across a variety
of quiz genres.

Then there are the social quizzers, that
hardcore of pub-quiz devotees whose
Tuesday night at the local is far more than
a good night out, it is a serious event where
ratings are carefully studied and proudly
achieved.

For those whose specialist subject is rugby union, *The Strangest Rugby Quiz Book* offers the chance to test their knowledge of the sport's more curious occasions from the past 150 years or so. Any individual or team performance that has been unusual, or events that have been clear departures from the ordinary, provide the backgrounds for the 25 categories that follow.

So, fingers on buzzers: here's your starter for ten.

John Griffiths

1

MEN AND WOMEN BEHAVING BADLY

Ale has been a part of rugby tradition since William Webb Ellis wrote an ode to the amber nectar more than 150 years ago. Fuelled by alcohol, players and spectators have sometimes had to take responsibility for high jinks that they have later regretted. Not that all rugby-related bad behaviour has been ale-induced. Some overstepping the mark have been stone-cold sober when acting out of character, incensed by events on the pitch, egged on perhaps by a wager or just carried away by youthful exuberance.

1 **WHO** were responsible for causing damage to the tune of £1,000 to the Calcutta Cup after a Saturday-night Edinburgh kick-about?

2 **WHO** was dropped from a winning Welsh team in 2010 after taking a golf buggy on a Sunday-morning jaunt along the M4?

3 **WHICH** rugby-playing member of the British royal family attracted unwanted tabloid headlines after visiting a dwarf-throwing event while he was a member of an England World Cup squad?

4 **WHOSE** Twickenham half-time display interrupted an England team talk given by Bill Beaumont?

5 **WHICH** Six Nations team in 2018 showed that high jinks among international players were alive and well more than 20 years after top-tier rugby entered its professional era?

6 **HOW** did a Scottish rugby supporter startle viewers of BBC Wales's early-evening news bulletin on the eve of the 2010 Wales-Scotland Six Nations match?

7 **WHAT** practice did Australian Michael O'Brien launch at Twickenham during a 1974 England-Wales charity match?

8 **WHY** was 56-year-old mother-of-two Hilda Madsen removed from the field during the France-South Canterbury tour match at Oamaru in 1961?

9 The unruly behaviour of spectators at **WHICH** Five Nations match in 1913 led to a temporary suspension of the fixture?

10 **HOW** did New Zealander William McKenzie 'con' spectators when he was dismissed during the New Zealand-New South Wales encounter in Sydney in July 1893?

'He radiated the fun and fellowship of rugby football as no other man I know.'

Tony O'Reilly's tribute to the Oxford University, Barbarians and England flanker of the 1950s, Peter Robbins.

THE ANSWERS 78

2

FAMOUS FOR 15 MINUTES

Various personalities have lived up to Andy Warhol's words, leaving their mark on rugby during short-lived spells in the limelight. These shooting stars include some known, slightly disparagingly, as 'one-cap wonders'. But who wouldn't give their right arm to say they won a match, made an influential decision, or even played just the once for their country?

1 Eric Tindill won his only cap for the All Blacks in their game against England in 1936, but **WHAT** is his unique sporting claim to fame?

2 The West Wales schoolmaster Denzil Thomas gained his only cap against Ireland in 1954. **HOW** did he win the match in the last minute?

3 **HOW** did the Dorchester Gladiators, an occasional team of rugby enthusiasts, enjoy 15 minutes of rugby fame during a charity visit to Romania at Easter, 2000?

4 **WHAT** coincidence connects the South African one-Test players Darius Botha and Stanley Osler?

• •

5 Otto Nothling set what was, at the time, a record for consecutive Test appearances for Australia in the 1920s, appearing 19 times in a row as a full-back/centre when rugby was confined at state level to New South Wales. **HOW** did he achieve fleeting international fame in another sport, and which Australian sporting great did he displace?

6 **WHO** was the Welsh rugby administrator who converted rugby from its sham-amateur ways into a professional sport in a single momentous meeting in Paris in 1995?

• •

7 **HOW** did French No. 8 Albert Cigagna earn a footnote in Test history at the 1995 Rugby World Cup?

8 **WHOSE** only Test tries in a brief international career were part of a rare 13-0 England win against New Zealand?

• •

9 **HOW** did Rodolphe Modin make his mark as an international player at the 1987 Rugby World Cup?

10 **WHAT** oversight by England's selectors led to Arnold Alcock winning a sole cap against South Africa in 1906?

THE ANSWERS 81

3

SHAKESPEAREAN CHARACTERS

The play's the thing, with characters from the Bard's works providing the theme for this collection of questions.

1 Sampson and Gregory are servants to Capulet in *Romeo and Juliet*, but for **WHICH** top-flight English club did they play in the 1990s?

2 **WHICH** country did the Prince of Denmark captain in the International Championship during the early years of the 20th century?

3 **NAME** the Archbishop of Canterbury in *King Henry VIII* who shared his name with an England captain of the 1930s.

4 **WHICH** recent Argentinian three-quarter holds in common a surname with the hero of *As You Like It*?

5 The title of **WHICH** of the Bard's histories was also the nickname coined by New Zealanders for the Lions fly-half who tormented them in 1971?

6 **WHAT** was the family name of the father and son both capped by Wales as hookers in the first half of the 20th century? They shared their name with the Earl of Northumberland's retainer in *Henry IV, Part Two*.

7 In **WHAT** sense is M. Duncan, who played for Scotland in 1888, unique among international rugby players?

8 **WHICH** Scottish hooker capped between the wars possessed the name of the Count of Roussillon in *All's Well That Ends Well*?

9 **WHICH** Tier One nation's list of international players includes surnames that chime with both the King of Naples and the daughter of Prospero in *The Tempest*?

10 **WHICH** of *The Two Gentlemen of Verona* had a name in common with an Australian scrum-half capped between 2006 and 2009, a pair of Scottish loose forwards who were internationalists in the post-Second World War years and an England three-quarter of the 1890s who died in unusual circumstances?

THE ANSWERS 85

4

CAPTAIN'S LOG

It's the perennial puzzle for any international team's selectors: do you pick your best 15 players first and then choose your captain, or do you select the skipper and build your starting 15 around the captain? It is a conundrum that has hatched some fascinating tales.

1 **HOW** did Eddie Jones break new ground when nominating his skipper for England's 2017 autumn Test against Samoa at Twickenham?

2 **WHO** was named as England's youngest captain for nearly 50 years when he was appointed by head coach, Geoff Cooke, to take charge of the team for the November 1988 Test against Australia at Twickenham?

3 The side now recognised as the first Lions team to venture overseas was the class of 1888 led by Lancastrian Bob Seddon. **WHY** was an empty seat left for him in the team photograph taken before the Lions met Queensland in Brisbane?

• •

4 **HOW** did Wales set a unique captaincy record when winning their first Grand Slam in 1908?

5 **WHOSE** unusual international career in the 1960s embraced 14 Test caps for his country, all as captain?

• •

6 **WHAT** difficult decisions did Mike Campbell-Lamerton (leading the Lions in New Zealand in 1966) and John Thornett (in charge of Australia in Europe later the same year) have to make as Test captains?

7 **WHAT** special honours as England captains do Albert 'Monkey' Hornby and Andrew 'Drewy' Stoddart share?

• •

8 Dawie de Villiers and Nelie Smith were South Africa's captain and vice-captain respectively for the Springboks tour of Australia and New Zealand in 1965. Richard Astre and Jacques Fouroux fulfilled those roles for France in South Africa ten years later. **WHAT** was unusual about the positions these players occupied on the field?

9 The autocratic Jean Prat was in charge of France in 1955. **HOW** did his prop, Amédée Domenech, react to the skipper's leadership when suddenly finding himself in possession during a passage of loose play against England at Twickenham?

10 **WHAT** was unusual about Theo Pienaar's captaincy record of the first Springboks to tour New Zealand in 1921?

'When in doubt, the referee is justified in deciding against the side which makes most noise. They are probably in the wrong.'

Dr H.H. Almond recalling his decision to allow a try by Scotland against protesting Englishmen in the 1871 international match.

THE ANSWERS 88

5

LONDON CALLING

Actually – with apologies to The Clash – it is London and the Home Counties that are the sources for these teasers.

1 **WHAT** significance does Kennington Oval have in England's rugby history?

2 **WHICH** Home Counties market town became an unlikely rugby Mecca in the 1990s thanks to the businessman Nigel Wray?

3 **WHERE** is 'Billy Williams's Cabbage Patch'?

4 **WHICH** is the only London ground other than Twickenham that has staged an official home rugby Test for England since 1910?

5 **WHICH** role did the Princess of Wales play in 1881 when the Welsh international rugby team made its maiden visit to London?

6 **WHAT** special rugby event took place at London's White City in 1908?

7 **WHICH** London sports club, now synonymous with racket sports, was once the venue for the annual Oxford-Cambridge Varsity rugby match?

8 **WHAT** phenomenon peculiar to London caused the double postponement of the 1890–91 Varsity match?

9 **HOW** did the London Counties enjoy a moment in rugby's limelight thanks to the goal-kicking of the son of a former London footballer in November 1951?

10 **WHICH** 'London' club is now based in Coventry?

THE ANSWERS 91

CONNECT THREE

Life's rich tapestry is decorated with patterns and coincidences, and rugby, arguably, is a microcosm of life itself. So what are the common denominators linking the seemingly random trios listed here?

1 Dr James Marsh (debut for Scotland 1889), Des Connor (Australia 1958) and Shane Howarth (New Zealand 1994).

2 Neyland RFC, Neath RFC and New Zealand.

3 Frederic Stokes (England 1871), the Hon. Francis Moncreiff (Scotland 1871) and Harry Watkins (Wales 1904).

4 Martin Donnelly (England 1947), Clive van Ryneveld (England 1949) and Kim Elgie (Scotland 1954–55).

• •

5 New Zealanders Jim Tilyard, Cliff Porter and Colin Meads.

6 C.H. (Howard) Davies (born in 1916 and capped by Wales in 1939 and 1947), D.N. (Dave) Grimmond (born in 1943 and capped by Australia in 1964), and N.C. (Nigel) Starmer-Smith (born in 1944 and capped by England in 1970 and 1971).

• •

7 Joe Worsley of England, Jason White of Scotland and J-P Pietersen of South Africa.

8 The three fleet-footed England wings Prince Alex Obolensky, Rory Underwood and his brother Tony.

• •

9 Rod Kafer, Doug Howlett and Brad Thorn, who all played professional rugby for both northern and southern hemisphere outfits.

10 Glen Jackson, Alain Rolland and Bob McMullen.

7

ORIGINS OF THE GAME

A form of football, the collective name for the modern games known as rugby, soccer, Gaelic, Aussie Rules, gridiron and others, is thought to have been played by the Chinese 4,000 years ago, and typically both the ancient Greeks and Romans had their words for recreations that loosely resembled it. In Britain, holiday celebrations involving the kicking of a ball date from the Middle Ages, but it was not until the early 19th century, at Rugby School in Warwickshire, that the defining elements of today's 15-a-side sport – handling, getting a try and scoring goals by kicking the ball *over* a crossbar – evolved, marking the true beginnings of Rugby football.

1 **WHO** is credited on a plaque at Rugby School with 'originating the distinctive feature of the Rugby game' by becoming, in 1823, the first footballer to gather the ball and run with it?

2 Bethlehem is to Christianity as Christ's College, Finchley, London, is to **WHICH** nation where rugby is nothing short of a religion?

---

3 **WHICH** country's first recorded rugby match, between university students in 1874, resulted in an upsurge of interest in the game among other college students and the formation of an inter-collegiate association two years later?

• •

4 **WHERE** was interest in rugby ignited by a demonstration match between visitors representing the famous Paris club, Racing, and Servette FC of Switzerland?

---

5 **WHICH** nation competing nowadays in the annual Rugby Championship traces its rugby origins back to 1873, when a group of British civil engineers based in the country's capital adopted the game as their main football code?

• •

6 The Catholic Marist Brothers brought the game to Samoa at the turn of the 19th and 20th centuries, but it was not until 1914, when expat New Zealanders persuaded their Union at home to provide proper leather balls, that rugby became the Islanders' national sport. **WHAT** did their players use in matches before that?

7 **WHICH** two Tier One nations' oldest clubs were founded at the countries' oldest universities in the 1850s and 1860s?

---

8 Rugby had been adopted in the Cape as part of Britain's colonial legacy by the 1870s, but **WHICH** African nation followed South Africa's lead and adopted the game in 1890?

• •

9 Ginnosuke Tanaka, who had enthusiastically embraced rugby football while studying at Cambridge University, established **WHICH** country's first rugby club in 1899?

---

10 In **WHICH** country did a group of theology students known as 'The Fighting Parsons' take part in the nation's first known match under Rugby School rules?

THE ANSWERS 99

8

UNEXPECTED INTERRUPTIONS

It's not that long ago that an international match kicking off at 2.30pm on a Saturday afternoon could be done and dusted by 4pm. Hard to believe, isn't it? But in the days before Television Match Officials and their replays, and when teams had only a quick breather for an on-field lemon at half-time, post-match celebrations could begin within an hour and a half of the game starting. Occasionally, however, unusual circumstances interrupted matches, causing them to overrun.

1 **HOW** did the long arm of the law intervene during a tightly contested match between the 1959 British & Irish Lions and Wanganui in New Zealand?

2 **WHAT** unique action did Scottish referee Jack Taylor take on his international refereeing debut controlling the Wales and Ireland clash at Cardiff in 1957?

3 **WHAT** match essential was in such short supply during the 1958 Wallabies' fixture with Midland Counties at Coventry's Highfield Road that play had to be halted for more than five minutes?

• •

4 **HOW** did a stray dog on Parker's Piece in Cambridge hold up the 1873 Varsity match?

5 **WHY** did a Volvo – a green one, of course – break the concentration of the London Irish team during a tense finish to their 1996 RFU Cup semi-final tie with Leicester Tigers?

• •

6 Only twice have Test matches involving Tier One nations been abandoned. The 1885 match between Ireland and Scotland in Belfast was called off after 30 minutes owing to torrential rain that flooded the pitch. **WHY** was the second Test of France's 1991 tour of the United States called off at half-time?

• •

7 **WHY** was the Aberavon-Bristol match of October 2013 abandoned after 70 minutes with the visitors leading 24-20?

8 **WHY** were a number of players forced to take an early shower during the Barbarians-Samoa match at London's Olympic Stadium in August 2015?

9 **WHO** was the Irish referee attacked by a lunatic South African supporter during a Tri-Nations Test at Durban in 2002?

---

10 **WHY** did Welsh referee Clive Norling offer to abandon the final Test of the 1981 series between New Zealand and South Africa in Auckland?

• •

'He always had a weak hand-off.'

Quote attributed to his school gamesmaster on hearing of the death in Nyasaland of Denys Dobson (England and British & Irish Lions) from wounds inflicted by a charging rhinoceros.

• •

THE ANSWERS 102

9

NICKNAMES

If there were a Rugby World Cup for nicknames alone, there is no doubt that South Africa would win hands down every time. Where else could you find such expressive nomens as 'The Beast' (as in Mtawarira) or Chiliboy (as in Ralepelle) on the team sheet? Let's face it, the shortened forms of some of England's recent enforcers – Deano, Lol or Johnno for instance – sound insipid in comparison with the expressive 'Boks. Fortunately, though, the Springboks don't have a complete monopoly of the best nicknames in rugby.

1 There was one Lancashire, England and Lions lock of the late 1980s and early 1990s who definitely was intimidating and had a tag to match. He was known as 'The Blackpool Tower', but **HOW** was he listed in match-day programmes?

2 Trains have been the inspiration for many wingers' nicknames. **WHICH** steam locomotive gave its name to the legendary Scottish wing Ian Smith who, between the wars, set what was then a world record for most tries scored in a Test career?

3 **WHICH** French wing, a recent member of their national coaching set-up, was known as 'The Bayonne Express'?

4 'The Bayonne Express' scored playing on the left-wing against England in Paris in 1990. **WHAT** tongue-in-cheek nickname was applied to all-round good egg and distinguished academic Mark Bailey, who occupied the corresponding position for the opposition?

5 Nicknames are obligatory for South African rugby players, even if born outside the republic. Bill Townsend, only the second Welsh-born Springbok, was inevitably nicknamed 'Taffy' when he won his sole Test cap for South Africa in New Zealand in 1921. But **WHAT** predictable soubriquet was given to Jack Partridge, the first Welshman capped by South Africa, in 1903?

6 **WHICH** Welsh flanker was called 'The Shadow' and for what reason?

7 Arthur Gould, who played for Wales between 1885 and 1897, was the Principality's first rugby superstar. But **WHY** was he called 'Monkey'?

8 **WHO** respectfully renamed Scottish prop Ian McLauchlan 'Mighty Mouse' in the light of the rugby events of 26 June 1971?

9 **WHY** was Australia's 1999 Rugby World Cup-winning captain John Eales called 'Nobody' by his team-mates?

10 France has enjoyed a reputation for turning out some of rugby's most talented dropped-goal kickers, but **WHO** is the only *Tricolore* recognised as 'Monsieur Drop?'

THE ANSWERS 106

10

MORE NAME GAMES

South African rugby players provide more examples of loose connections between names. Marx and Bismarck, in their different ways, were political giants of the 19th century, but they were also two outstanding Springbok hookers of recent times: Bismarck du Plessis and Malcolm Marx. So, broadly speaking, what's in a name?

1 Newport-born Charles G. Jordan had the unusual distinction of turning out for Ireland when they were short for their international match with Wales at Cardiff Arms Park in April 1884. After **WHICH** general, heavily involved with the unification of Italy, was he named?

2 And **WHO** who was the French statesman and military leader from whom Charles N. Kingstone, New Zealand's full-back in their first encounter with the Springboks in 1921, took his second chosen name?

3 Holmes and Moriarty were fictional adversaries created by Sir Arthur Conan Doyle, but **WHO** were the larger-than-life adversaries with the same names in Cardiff–Swansea club matches during the first half of the 1980s?

4 Cyril Joynson was a well-known Welsh referee in the 1950s. Born on 1 March 1912, **WHAT** patriotic first name was he given by his parents?

5 According to one definition, nominative determinism is the theory that people tend to gravitate towards areas of work that fit their names. **HOW** could that have been said to be true of a loose forward capped by Wales in the early 1950s?

6 Between 1935 and 1949, Wales capped only two scrum-halves in official Tests. Both were christened with the names of famous composers. **WHO** were they?

7 Arguably there can be no greater compliment to a rugby player than to name your son after him, as Ireland's Mick Leahy did after watching Wilson Whineray's Fifth All Blacks of 1963. **WHO** was the honoured New Zealand forward?

8 **WHO** was the 1959 Lions full-back who shared his name with the Home Union for which he was capped 27 times between 1957 and 1965?

● ●

9 Edward V. Watkins, the Cardiff and Wales forward of the mid- to late 1930s, was born in 1916 shortly after the beginning of one of the longest and bloodiest battles of the Great War. **WHAT** was his second name?

10 The Irish back-rower Colm Tucker became used to seeing his name spelt in the English press as Colin Tucker. But **HOW** did a French printer get his name spectacularly wrong in Paris in 1980?

THE ANSWERS ☞ 109

BRAINTEASERS

If simultaneous equations, relative velocity, geometry theorems or explanations that begin 'let x be the unknown ...' summon up unhappy memories of daily maths lessons, then move along now: there's nothing to see here. However, if the odd puzzle requiring a bit of mathematical savvy or logical thinking appeals, read on, pencil and paper at the ready.

1 **WHY** do New Zealand call their inside-centre/fly-half pair 'five-eighths'?

2 The 2013 Six Nations was a tournament that went to the wire. On the last weekend of the championship, Wales not only needed to beat England to edge the title, they also had to win by a significant margin to overtake England's superior points difference. Before the match, Wales had scored 92 points and conceded 63, compared to England's 91 for and 48 against. So **WHAT** was the minimum winning margin Wales required to be certain of claiming the title?

3 At the time of publication, Dan Carter, Andrew Mehrtens and Grant Fox were New Zealand's leading points-scorers in Tests. Carter and Mehrtens combined totalled 2,565 points, Mehrtens and Fox 1,612, and Fox and Carter together, 2,243. **WHAT** were the individual points scored by the three players?

4 When Wales played England at Cardiff in 1893, the crowd left the ground believing that the match had been drawn 14-all under the experimental scoring values operating in Welsh club matches at the time. The Welsh scored three tries, converted one and landed a penalty goal; England crossed for four tries and converted one. Given that each scoring action was worth either two or three points, **WHAT** were the values of: i) a try; ii) a conversion; and iii) a penalty?

5 The International Board, however, had recently ruled that scoring values should be uniform for international matches and laid down their own points system. As a result, Wales won 12-11. **WHAT** were the values for: i) a try; ii) a conversion; and iii) a penalty under the Board's system?

6 **WHEN** is a forward pass *not* a forward pass?

7 **WHERE'S** the best position to take a conversion from when a try has been scored? (Assume that kicking range, elevation and weather conditions can be neglected.)

---

8 If H = 1, I = 2 and J = 3, **WHAT** was A at the 1988 RFU Cup Final between Bristol and Harlequins at Twickenham?

• •

9 The former Five Nations involved the four Home Unions and France meeting each other in a round-robin tournament – i.e. each team played each other team once. Two championship points were awarded for winning, one for drawing a game, and none for losing. One season the table finished as follows:

Wales – 7 points
Ireland – 6 points
England – 4 points
Scotland – 2 points
France –1 point

Given there was only one drawn match, **DEDUCE** the outcomes of every match.

---

10 **WHAT** *could* have been the most draws in the tournament that would have given the same final points listed in the previous question?

THE ANSWERS 112

12

TROPHY CABINET

Mad dogs and Englishmen might well have gone out in the midday sun during the days of the British Raj, but they didn't go out to play rugby – or not in Calcutta after 1878. That was the year the local club, after its five-year existence, was disbanded owing to dwindling numbers and lack of interest. The club's funds, comprising a stash of rupees, were melted down, transformed into a trophy and presented to the RFU in London. The Union decided to brand it the 'Calcutta Cup', with the intention of presenting it as the reward to the winners of the annual England-Scotland international match – the oldest Test fixture on the rugby calendar. It thus became the first material prize for any international rugby fixture, though the inaugural match for the Cup, in 1879, was a draw, so it remained under wraps until England became its maiden winners a year later. Today, there is a tangible trophy up for grabs when most of the Tier One nations meet.

1 **WHICH** trophy is played for between the Test teams of New Zealand and Australia?

2 Wales and Australia compete for the James Bevan Trophy, but **WHAT** was his connection with the two nations?

3 **WHAT** reward of a distinct Viking helmet design was first awarded for matches between Ireland and England in 1988?

4 **WHICH** perpetual Test series is played for the Cook Cup?

5 **WHO** are the northern/southern hemisphere Test rivals who compete for the Dave Gallaher Trophy?

6 **NAME** the countries that are pitted against each other for the Hillary Shield.

7 According to tradition, New Zealand and South Africa enjoy the most intense rugby rivalry on the planet, but **WHAT** are the spoils for the winners of Test matches between rugby's two great superpowers?

8 In the Test series for **WHICH** Plate do all squad members of one team wear the number 46664?

9 **WHICH** countries are matched for the Lansdowne Cup?

10 **NAME** the Home Union that is the common factor in the Hopetoun Cup, the Centenary Quaich and the Auld Alliance Trophy?

'I knew a woman from Taibach who before a home match at Aberavon used to drop goals from around 40 yards with either foot to entertain the crowd.'

Actor and rugby fanatic Richard Burton recalling his Welsh childhood.

THE ANSWERS 117

THE NUMBERS GAME

A Buggles re-release might go, 'Internet Killed the Reference Book' – especially in sport. Back in the day, sports buffs fascinated themselves poring over almanacs or yearbooks crammed with sporting records and trivia. Names such as Playfair, Wisden, Guinness and Rothmans evoke memories of sporting bibles that sent readers meandering along pathways where one random fact led to myriad others. Many sporting numbers became stamped on the memory, such as Len Hutton's 364 runs against Australia at The Oval in 1938, which remains an England Test record. And what about the 3 minutes 59.4 seconds that defined Sir Roger Bannister's barrier-breaking time for the mile he ran at Oxford's Iffley Road in May 1954? **WHAT** significance do these numbers have in rugby? (Clues in brackets.)

1 0 (Last scoreless Test.)

2 8 (Position on the field.)

3 17 (Successive Test defeats.)

● ●

4 18-19 (Famous late defeat.)

_____

5 18 (Test winning run.)

● ●

6 30 (Famous crowd number.)

_____

7 53 (His entire national Test career.)

● ●

8 148 (Appearance record.)

_____

9 1,598 (Individual Test record.)

● ●

10 109,874 (Another notable crowd.)

THE ANSWERS ☞ 120

QUOTE, UNQUOTE

Down the years, rugby has been blessed with more than its fair share of wits and jokers. From Dr Almond, umpire at the first international match in 1871, to the luminaries of the new millennium, there has been no shortage of colourful characters ever ready to add the odd *bon-mot* or two to rugby's rich legends. Dr Almond set this particular ball rolling when, commenting on England objecting vociferously to one of his rulings in the sport's inaugural Test match in 1871, memorably judged: 'When in doubt, I think [the referee] is justified in deciding against the side which makes the most noise. They are probably in the wrong.'

WHAT were the contexts in which these quotes were made?

1 'One of the greatest moments in New Zealand swimming.'

2 'I seem to have turned wine into water.'

3 'He's awesome, a freak and the sooner he goes away the better.'

• •

4 'Either you stop this fighting or I'll abandon the game.'

5 'Look, Gar, you throw it, I'll catch it.'

• •

6 'Same as usual: low and crooked.'

7 'He was in a bad way. Mind, he smelled lovely.'

• •

8 In **WHICH** of the Home Unions was the state of rugby described as: 'Hopeless, but never serious.'

9 'I certainly hope not.'

• •

10 'In his capacity as a wholesale butcher, Thomas was one of the few people able to take his weekday work with him on to the rugby field at weekends.'

THE ANSWERS 123

15

POLITICAL CONNECTIONS

Politicians have often courted publicity by appearing at sporting events and rugby is no exception to visits from celebrated statesmen. Climbing politics' greasy pole in 1907, David Lloyd-George declared rugby to be 'a most extraordinary game – more exciting than politics', while his party ally, H.H. Asquith, looked to enhance his reputation as Prime Minister by attending the 1914 England-Ireland international at Twickenham when his Parliament was debating the thorny issue of Irish Home Rule. Éamon de Valera, too, was a regular visitor to Dublin's Lansdowne Road to see rugby, the sport that uniquely united the north and south of a troubled land, during his long Presidency of the Republic. How many of these who were famous in international rugby *before* beating a political path can you identify?

1 **NAME** the referee who regularly whistled on the London circuit in the 1950s before becoming the consort of a British Prime Minister.

2 **WHO** was the most recent England international player to run successfully for Parliament?

• •

3 **WHICH** full-back of the 1970s led the Republic of Ireland Labour Party from 1982 to 1997?

4 Clem Thomas was a Welsh flanker and captain in the 1950s who was later a distinguished rugby journalist, but for **WHICH** British political party was he a Parliamentary candidate at the 1974 and 1979 General Elections?

• •

5 And **WHO** was Clem's contemporary, a fellow Welsh international, friend and journalist, who contested Llanelli at the 1970 General Election as the Plaid Cymru candidate?

6 **WHO** was the French rugby international who served as Prime Minister under Georges Pompidou between 1969 and 1972?

• •

7 The 1967 All Blacks team that toured Britain and France included three players who later sat as MPs in New Zealand's Parliament. **WHO** were they?

8 **WHICH** Springbok scrum-half between 1962 and 1970 went into politics after ordination as a minister in the Dutch Reform Church?

9 **WHO** set an England appearance record that stood for more than 40 years, was the first player to insist that his forwards packed in specialist positions at scrums and sat as a Conservative MP from 1935 until 1963?

10 **WHERE** did Trevor Ringland, a 1980s Five Nations regular, stamp his mark in politics?

THE ANSWERS 126

16

BUSINESS MATTERS

As he reaches the end of his marathon career at the top of professional rugby's highly competitive tree, the England and Lions forward James Haskell, in common with other rugby players whose careers are at a similar stage, is thinking about his immediate future; what to do next after leaving the playing stage. In a recent interview he said he wants to become an entrepreneur but that his motivation was a passion for business rather than making shedloads of money. If he brings to business the same qualities of commitment and dedication he has shown to rugby, then he has every chance of following in the footsteps of several predecessors who successfully made the transition.

1 Rugby's most successful player-turned-businessman in the amateur era was the former Ireland and Lions three-quarter Tony O'Reilly, who regularly featured in lists of the world's richest men. **WHICH** well-known American food organisation did he head while still playing first-class rugby?

2 **WHO** was the Scottish internationalist who became an oil millionaire after founding the Cairn Energy company?

● ●

3 Slazenger have been well-known sports outfitters for more than a century, but for **WHICH** country did one of the company's founding brothers play international rugby in the 1880s?

4 J.E. 'Jenny' Greenwood was England's first captain after the Great War, but of **WHICH** major company was he a director from 1920 to 1953, retiring as its vice-chairman?

● ●

5 **NAME** the England and Lions prop who set up and ran the thriving eponymous clothing business that specialises in mail order.

6 And **WHICH** of his contemporaries in England and Lions front rows built a successful business in the fields of corporate hospitality as well as carving a niche for himself as a travel agent specialising in sporting trips?

● ●

7 **IDENTIFY** the Australian Union forward of Lebanese descent who made two tours of Britain, Ireland and France ten years apart before prospering in the commercial and public affairs of his home city, Sydney.

8 Nigel Wray's hard-earned wealth has bankrolled Saracens for more than two decades, transforming the club from one of London's Cinderella outfits into arguably the leading Premiership team in the land. But **WHICH** rugby club did he turn out for in his playing days, and for which county did he feature in the County Championship competition?

---

9 **WHO** is the household rugby name, a former England Grand Slam captain and now Chairman of World Rugby, who remains managing director of the family textiles manufacturing business in Lancashire?

• •

10 **WHICH** two iconic All Blacks skippers, one from the early 1960s and the other a Rugby World Cup-winning captain, successfully transferred their leadership skills to business, the elder as chairman of a major New Zealand company and the younger as head of the Fairfax media group?

THE ANSWERS 129

17

HALL
OF FARMERS

'Eat-Sleep-Farm-Repeat' it says on a T-shirt that is popular in the British agricultural community. It sums up the treadmill that is modern farming. Equally, modern rugby forwards could justifiably describe their workload as 'Ruck-Maul-Drive-Repeat', with perhaps the odd scrum or line-out as variation. The physical and temperamental demands of the agricultural business cuts farmers out for forward play on the rugby field, so how many of these famous Hall of Farmers can you recall?

1 **WHICH** Bristol hooker won distinction as the first man to captain England to victories over South Africa, New Zealand and Australia?

2 The noted Neath front row of Brian Williams, Kevin Phillips and John Davies played together for Wales in the early 1990s, but in **WHICH** Welsh county did all three run thriving farms?

3 Headingley's Jack King enlisted for service within days of the declaration of war in August 1914, leaving his siblings to run the family farm. But **WHAT** England forward record does the dozen times capped farmer Jack hold?

4 **WHO** was the Scotland and Lions prop of the 1960s who put his strength and fitness down to his daily farming routine of heaving sacks of feed and potatoes?

5 **WHICH** New Zealander's legendary upper-body strength was attributed to his habit of carrying sheep under each arm on his hill farm?

6 **WHO** was the cattle farmer who, in 1937, became the first Springbok captain to lead a winning side in a series between New Zealand and South Africa?

7 According to All Black legend Bryan Williams, **WHO** was the best all-round New Zealand skipper of the six he played under?

8 A farming son of a Borders farmer, **WHO** was the Scottish flanker responsible in 1949 and 1951 for wreaking havoc among the Welsh half-backs and helping lay the foundations for famous Murrayfield wins?

9 'Farmers make the finest flankers' could well have been the motto of the Scottish selectors. **WHO** was the Borders loose forward they chose to fill a key role in the famous 13-7 win against England at Murrayfield in 1990, when Scotland claimed the Grand Slam?

10 Ricky Bartlett, the fly-half who spearheaded England's back division in the late 1950s, is the exception to the forward theme in this final question. **WHAT** was his particular animal husbandry specialism?

'I'm not really partisan. I don't care who wins as long as Ireland doesn't get beat.'

Irish comedian Dave Allen.

THE ANSWERS 132

18

AUTHOR! AUTHOR!

Players pocketing fees or royalties from writing about rugby were once regarded as committing a crime tantamount to treason in the eyes of the International Board (later World Rugby). The union game's strict amateur code prohibited players or officials making any gain from involvement in rugby, including the writing of articles or books. As a result, players publishing autobiographies were condemned as outcasts and banned from putting something back into the game. Fortunately for readers hungry for the inside track on rugby union, many ex-internationals reaching the twilight of their playing days were happy to forfeit their amateur status by taking the proceeds of autobiographies, many of which provided fascinating insights into the life of the top-class international players, while many more followed suit when constraints were removed in the 1990s. So, how many famous players can you identify from these titles?

1 A Welsh Grand Slam winner and British & Irish Lion while still comfortably in his teens, **WHOSE** autobiography published in 1958 was entitled *King of Rugger*?

2 **WHO** was the Welshman who played union, went to league and, in the early days of the open game, made a successful return to union? He told the story of his career in *Code Breaker*, first published in 1996.

3 *Nine Lives*, published in 2004, was written by **WHICH** member of the 2003 England Rugby World Cup-winning team?

4 **WHICH** of his team-mates from the class of 2003 told his story in *Landing on my Feet*?

5 And to complete the feline trilogy, **WHOSE** life was described in *Top Cat*, which first appeared in its English-language version in 2002?

6 **WHOSE** memoirs, entitled *Beware of the Dog*, came out in 2010, 15 years after his original autobiography saw the light of day?

7 Published in 2006, *Centre of Excellence* told the story of **WHICH** long-serving Scottish player's career?

8 Hennie Muller was a pivotal member of the Springbok teams that whitewashed the All Blacks 4-0 in 1949, completed a Grand Slam over the Home Unions and France in 1951–52 and won a series against Australia the following year to claim the unofficial title of rugby's world champions. He told his story in *Tot Siens to Test Rugby* in 1953, but **WHAT** position on the field did he occupy?

9 The All Black who became infamous in Britain and Ireland for landing six penalties to defeat the Lions 18-17 in a Test at Dunedin in 1959 entitled his autobiography *The Boot*. **WHO** was he?

10 **WHO** told the story of his rugby career in *Rainbow Warrior* in 1999? As captain, he was the face of South Africa's 1995 Rugby World Cup win and was famously photographed holding the Cup with President Nelson Mandela wearing a replica of the skipper's No. 6 Springbok jersey.

THE ANSWERS 135

19

FAMILY TIES

Rugby prowess has been in the DNA of some families since the first international match in 1871. England forward Reg Birkett blazed the trail for his younger brother and son to follow, while six of the opposing Scottish team would see their brothers subsequently represent their country. Fast forward 147 years to the summer of 2018 and, for England, one finds Owen Farrell (son of former league and union international Andy) and among the Scots, Adam Hastings, offspring of Gavin and nephew of Scott, still maintaining family ties. In between, rugby has been graced by countless examples of relatives who have achieved international status.

1 **HOW** did Scotland's McClure brothers set a Test rugby precedent in the 1870s?

2 **HOW** did the Barrett brothers create New Zealand rugby history against France at Eden Park, Auckland, in June 2018?

3 **WHAT** honour is shared by the McLeans (Doug, Bill and Peter) of Australia and the Murphys (Noel senior, Noel junior and Kenny) of Ireland?

4 **WHICH** brothers displayed their talents across the sporting spectrum by winning selection in Test cricket and rugby sides for England on the same Saturdays in 1974?

5 Scotland's best-known international twins were Jim and Finlay Calder, who were also British & Irish Lions, but **WHAT** was unusual about their careers?

6 Some brothers entered the record-books playing Tests against one another. For **WHICH** countries were Mike and Tana Umaga in opposition in 1999?

7 **WHAT** family confrontation occurred for the first time at Test level when Ireland met England in Dublin during the 2017 Six Nations?

8 **WHAT** doubly unique record did the Ma'afu brothers create in the Australia-Fiji Test at Canberra in June 2010?

9 Ireland has capped more than 50 sets of brothers, but **HOW** many pairs lined up to face Wales in 1924?

10 **WHY** did Feidlim McLoughlin, the Irish prop of the 1970s, relish informing new acquaintances how he and his brother Ray played 41 times between them for Ireland?

'I like to get one really good tackle in early in the game – even if it's late.'

Crash-tackling Welsh centre Ray Gravell.

THE ANSWERS 138

20
IN THE LINE OF FIRE

Commemorations of both the First and Second World Wars have revealed the challenging situations many of sport's best-known players experienced during hostilities. Across both world wars rugby union players were among the quickest off the mark to serve, many of them distinguishing themselves through heroic deeds or being noted for other reasons. So it is the rugby community in the line of fire that provides the context for these questions.

1 **WHAT** wartime distinctions do the Irish rugby internationals Tom Crean, Robert Johnston and Frederick Harvey, and the England cap Arthur Harrison share?

2 Noel Chavasse played rugby for Liverpool College and was a member of the Trinity College, Oxford, Cuppers squad in 1907–08. **WHAT** was his unique Great War achievement?

3 And **HOW** did the New Zealander Charles Upham, who had played rugby for Canterbury Agricultural College, similarly distinguish himself in the Second World War?

• •

4 Among the First World War rugby casualties were the international players Ronnie Poulton and Freddie Turner, who were on opposing sides in the last international match staged on British soil before the conflict began. **WHAT** club did they both play for in 1914?

5 **WHO** was the Northampton and England three-quarter killed in action at Zillebeke in July 1917 whose name was commemorated by an annual Barbarians match?

• •

6 Blair Swannell, another Northampton 'Saint' killed in action during the First World War, played international rugby for both the British & Irish Lions and Australia. **WHERE** and on **WHAT** day of national significance to those down under did he meet his death?

7 **WHAT** unique sporting feat was achieved by Maurice Turnbull, the rugby international killed in Normandy in August 1944?

8 **NAME** the Ireland and Lions forward awarded the Distinguished Service Order (DSO) three times and the Légion d'Honneur in the Second World War.

• •

9 **HOW** was the rugby career of South African prop Okey Geffin shaped by his experiences in the Second World War?

___

10 John MacCallum was Scotland's most capped player and a distinguished former captain of the national side before the First World War, but **WHAT** stance did he take during the conflict that set him apart from his fellow rugby internationals?

THE ANSWERS 141

21

STAGE AND SCREEN

A news item that caught the eye in October 2018 announced that a movie about Japan's shock win against South Africa at the 2015 Rugby World Cup was in the offing. 'The Brighton Miracle', it continued, would tell the story behind the brilliant victory plan devised by manager Eddie Jones and perfectly executed by his Japanese underdogs. With that in mind, then, it's cue action! How many of these past stage and screen productions with rugby connections do you remember?

1 Colin Welland's Oscar-winning 1981 historical drama *Chariots of Fire* told the story of the athletes Eric Liddell and Harold Abrahams and their quests for gold at the 1924 Paris Olympics, but **WHICH** of the protagonists had a distinguished rugby union career?

2 **WHAT** was the rugby context of the 1992 film *Alive*, Frank Marshall's adaptation of Piers Paul Read's true story?

3 The actor Richard Todd played a host of parts that typified the British stiff upper lip during the 1950s, but for **WHICH** country did his father appear at full-back before the Great War?

4 **WHOSE** film-star good looks and dashing personality during the 1955 Lions tour of South Africa attracted the attention of film directors casting for the title role of *Ben-Hur*?

5 **WHO** was the Scotland and Lions three-quarter of the 1920s whose son and grandson became well-known stage and screen actors?

6 **WHAT** special day in Ireland's rugby history was celebrated in the stage play *Alone It Stands*?

7 **WHICH** 2009 film starring Morgan Freeman and Matt Damon related the events before and during the 1995 Rugby World Cup in South Africa?

8 **WHO** was the 1990s England and Lions rugby international who featured in the *Harry Potter* films as Robbie Coltrane's body double in the role of Hagrid?

9 **WHICH** popular long-running American sitcom series once featured a guest appearance by the 1986 and 1987 Cambridge University rugby Blue Mark Thomas?

10 **WHAT** was the title of the feature-length BBC Wales comedy about a group of Welsh supporters visiting Paris for a boozy Five Nations weekend in the 1970s?

'I prefer rugby to soccer. I enjoy the violence of rugby, except when they are biting each other's ears off.'

The actress Elizabeth Taylor reflecting on the rough Wales-England match at Cardiff in 1965, which she had attended with Richard Burton.

THE ANSWERS 144

22

FAMOUS FIRSTS AND LASTS

In the 1950s the most common questions handled by the Welsh national daily the *Western Mail*, when its daily circulation was in six figures, were 'Who was the last Welshman to drop a goal worth four points in an international and who was the first to drop one worth three points?', the value of the scoring action having changed in 1948. (Answers: Willie Davies against Ireland in 1939 and Billy Cleaver against Scotland in 1950.) Here are some more firsts and lasts to ponder.

1 The legendary Welsh full-back Billy Bancroft was the first to perform **WHICH** scoring action in an international match?

2 **WHAT** feat was M.J.K. (Mike) Smith the last rugby player to achieve?

3 **WHAT** historical significance surrounded Ireland's match against England in 2007?

4 **HOW** did the Welsh centre Jerry Shea's scoring create a Test first against England at Swansea in January 1920?

5 **WHAT** double-first did Scotland's Donna Kennedy accomplish in 2007?

6 Harry Frazer of New Zealand was the first player to register **WHICH** type of scoring action in a Test?

7 **HOW** has Scott Gibbs's try for Wales against England at Wembley in April 1999 gone down as one of rugby's most famous 'lasts'?

8 Named after the former *Daily Express* rugby writer, the Pat Marshall Memorial Award has been presented by the Rugby Union Writers' Club since 1975. **WHO** was the first woman to win this coveted award?

9 Billy Wallace (two against Australia in 1903) was the first, and Don Clarke (against England at Christchurch in 1963) was the last to score with **WHICH** type of action in Tests for New Zealand?

10 **HOW** did Scotland's 'Broons from Troon' – Peter and Gordon Brown – become Test firsts at Cardiff in 1970?

THE ANSWERS 147

23

BLOOPERS

Bloopers are defined as unintended indiscretions, real howlers that their perpetrators would like to expunge from their memories. Although they are usually associated with film and television, any blunder made in front of an audience can be called a blooper. Rugby players are particularly prone to such errors because of the nature of the game and the unpredictability of a bouncing oval ball.

1 **WHOSE** lapse of concentration in Port Elizabeth during the decisive third Test of the Lions-Springboks Test series in 1980 cost the British/Irish team the match and with it the rubber?

2 **WHAT** happened next when French wing Patrick Estève went over in the corner after a slick three-quarter movement against England at Twickenham in 1985?

3 **WHO** was the maverick Australian wing whose blunder when playing against the Lions in the final Test of the 1989 series presented Ieuan Evans with the try that sealed the series for the British/Irish team?

• •

4 **NAME** the Bath player whose premature celebration of a try blew his side's chances of winning a crucial European Champions Cup pool match at home to Toulouse in October 2018.

5 Referees haven't been exempt from bloopers at the highest level. **WHO** mistakenly awarded Gareth Edwards a dropped goal in Dublin in 1968 and nearly sparked off a riot?

• •

6 **WHAT** was perceived as a blunder by Welsh captain Terry Davies in the Wales-South Africa Test at Cardiff in 1960?

7 **HOW** did England captain Lawrence Dallaglio err in the closing minutes of England's Grand Slam bid against Wales at Wembley in April 1999?

• •

8 **WHICH** captain's aberration cost his side a draw in a tight 2015 Rugby World Cup pool match and effectively put paid to their chances of qualifying for the knockout stages?

9 **HOW** did English referee Ken Pattinson cause a stir when Andy Irvine kicked a long-range penalty goal for Scotland against France at Murrayfield in 1976?

---

10 **WHOSE** lack of awareness at a tense moment late in England's 1981 visit to Cardiff gifted Wales a match-winning penalty?

● ●

"What qualification have you got to play for England?"

Prince Edward (soon to be King Edward VIII) when presented to the exiled Russian Prince Alex Obolensky before the England-New Zealand match of 1936.

● ●

THE ANSWERS 150

24

RUG-LIT

Rugby fiction has never established itself as a recognised genre. Maybe the sport lacks the behind-the-scenes potential for threading the kind of plots that made Dick Francis's horse-racing tales so popular. And certainly rugby lacks the scope that cricket gives for the author to write contemplatively and descriptively about a game played at a leisurely pace. But more likely it's the dynamic nature of rugby and the speed with which situations change – the genuine unpredictability of a real match – that places it beyond the realms of engaging story-telling, but that is not to say that rugby has been completely overlooked in fiction.

1 **WHICH** British classic, first published in 1857, contains a detailed description of how rugby football was played in mid-Victorian times?

2 **WHICH** annual event on the rugby calendar is featured in A.G. Macdonell's wonderfully evocative *England, Their England* published in 1933?

3 **WHO** wrote the short story *The Ordeal of Young Tuppy*, in which the character Tuppy Glossop tries to impress a young lady friend by playing rugby?

4 In William Boyd's novel *Any Human Heart*, Logan Mountstuart remembers from his experiences of a school rugby scrum that 'Two packs would face each other, a 32-legged, human beetle trying to evacuate an oval leather ball.' **WHAT** position did he occupy?

5 **WHICH** popular children's fiction character gets roped in to play for the Peruvian Second XV in an adventure published in 1974?

6 **WHOSE** funny tales of lower-level rugby have become the game's best-selling titles?

7 **WHICH** rugby ground is the setting for the denouement to the crime writer Reginald Hill's *A Clubbable Woman?*

8 Heather Kidd, the well-known Kiwi writer and journalist, started her writing career as a rugby columnist whose bylines adorned a number of publications, including New Zealand's weekly *Rugby News*. A venture into fiction resulted in her 1984 novel *Operation Intercept*. **WHO** is kidnapped and which major rugby event is put in jeopardy?

• •

9 The name Thomas Nelson probably means little to today's rugby enthusiasts, but in the late 1890s he was a gifted Edinburgh Academicals centre who won Oxford Blues and played for Scotland against England in 1898. **WHICH** of his contemporaries, a well-known Scottish novelist and historian, dedicated his best-known adventure to Nelson?

• •

10 *The Book of Fame* is Lloyd Jones's fictional account of **WHICH** famous rugby tour?

THE ANSWERS ☞ 154

25

NEVER MIND THE WEATHER

Regulars at Cardiff Arms Park internationals in the late 1950s and early 1960s had probably the most diverse winter wardrobes of any rugby followers in the Five Nations. The vagaries of the Welsh climate meant that spectators on the old terraces and enclosures needed a wide range of outdoor clothing for protection against rain, frost, snow or whatever other freak conditions swept over the ground on big match days. Wales, though, doesn't own the exclusive rights to awful conditions for rugby matches. It is a tribute to ground staff all over the world that down the years their work ethic has always been that never mind the weather, the game goes on.

1 **WHY** did referee Jack Taylor offer to abandon the 1960 Wales-South Africa Test at Cardiff 15 minutes before the end of the match?

2 **WHAT** special kit were the Wales and England teams offered for their 1963 match at Cardiff?

3 **WHICH** touring side had to be airlifted by helicopter from their snow-bound Penarth hotel when the showpiece tour finale against the Barbarians in Cardiff was abandoned?

4 Cardiff isn't the only city where the weather has been noted for its lack of respect for rugby. **WHY** did the Irish captain have to leave the field prematurely during his team's match with Scotland in Dublin in 1927?

5 The last rugby international that took place at Inverleith in Edinburgh was Scotland's meeting with France in January 1925. For **WHAT** reason was the kick-off advanced ten minutes?

6 **WHY** was the 1908 England-Wales match at Bristol an almost complete mystery to the crowd?

7 **WHAT** novel idea was devised for lessening the ordeal of the players in the 1913 Test between New Zealand and Australia, which was staged in extremely wet and windy conditions in Wellington?

8 **WHAT** unusual experience was shared by the players in the 1885 Ireland-Scotland match in Belfast and those involved in the 1991 Test between the United States and France at Colorado Springs?

9 **HOW** did the San Isidro Rugby Club from Argentina spend the day of what should have been the first match of their tour to Britain in January 1963?

• •

10 Identical conditions affected the prospects of the France-Ireland Paris fixtures of 1978 and 2012, but in **WHAT** different ways were they dealt with by the French Rugby Union (FFR)?

• •
━━━━━━━━━━━━━━━━━━━━━━━━━━━━━━━━━━━━

'That was the greatest moment of my life.'

All Black hooker Bruce McLeod on receiving a congratulatory handshake on his Test call-up in 1964 from New Zealand great Colin Meads.

━━━━━━━━━━━━━━━━━━━━━━━━━━━━━━━━━━━━
• •

THE ANSWERS 156

★ THE ANSWERS ★

MEN AND WOMEN BEHAVING BADLY

1. The culprits were John Jeffrey (a Scottish reserve) and Dean Richards (England's No. 8) in the wake of the dire 1988 Scotland-England match. The traditional post-match dinner had been boisterous, with large quantities of alcohol consumed before the pair incredibly managed to smuggle the ancient trophy onto the streets of Edinburgh for an impromptu replay of the afternoon's match. One wit later revealed that forthwith the Calcutta Cup was to be known as the Calcutta Plate. Both players subsequently received bans, but the Scottish Union's main concern was how the duo had managed to spirit the trophy onto the streets of the capital without any official's knowledge.

2. Andy Powell had had a few sherbets too many celebrating Wales's last-minute 31-24 win against Scotland when the next morning he hijacked a golf buggy from the hotel where the Welsh side were quartered and embarked on an epic ride along country lanes and a section of the M4. When police arrested him he immediately admitted his guilt and failed a breathalyser. 'I'm an idiot, I know,' he told the arresting officer, and later remarked to a reporter: 'I've done stupid things before but nothing like this.' It was a costly brush with the law. He was fined £1,000, given a 15-month driving ban and expelled from Warren Gatland's Wales squad.

3. Mike Tindall, who had only recently married the Princess Royal's daughter, Zara Phillips, was at the centre of a controversy during England's disappointing 2011 Rugby World Cup campaign in New Zealand. After leading his

country to a pool-match win over Argentina he was reported drunk, allegedly in the presence of a female friend, at a Mad Midget Weekender event in a Queenstown bar. There was no need to juice up a story that was the stuff of dreams for tabloid newspaper editors. Tindall, a member of England's 2003 Rugby World Cup-winning team and an integral part of their set-up for the best part of a decade, never played Test rugby again after that 2011 tournament.

4. It was Erika Roe, whose spectacular topless appearance at the 1982 England-Australia match caused England players' attentions to wander far from the half-time exhortations of their captain. The 24-year-old from Petersfield was not the first streaker at a rugby international, but she remains the sport's most famous one.

5. France. Eight members of the side that was beaten 32-26 at Murrayfield in February 2018 broke a team curfew to go out on the town after slipping to an eighth successive Test defeat. The miscreants were subsequently suspended by the French Rugby Federation after Scottish police delayed their flight home the next day to investigate an alleged offence, though no criminal charges were brought.

6. Rugby supporter Keith Davies, visiting Wales with Hawick RFC, dropped his kilt and exposed himself on the channel's teatime news programme *Wales Today* as it opened its bulletin live from Glynneath RFC. The programme's sports presenter was preparing her introductions with assembled guests before hosting a match preview when the young Scot carried off one of the most outrageous stunts ever broadcast.

7. He started the craze for streaking at international matches. A photographer captured him for posterity as he was escorted along the Twickenham sideline by a bobby who had covered up O'Brien's embarrassment with a strategically placed police helmet. He was taken to the local police station where

he was charged and swiftly released – so swiftly, in fact, that legend has it that he returned to the ground and saw the last 20 minutes of the match.

8. Mrs Madsen had attacked French loose forward Michel Crauste on the pitch. The Frenchman had flattened South Canterbury's Eddie Smith with a stiff-arm tackle before compounding his offence by cynically picking the player up by the scruff of the neck and dropping him back to the ground. Incensed, the Oamaru mother-of-two, who was attending the match with her family, ran onto the pitch to remonstrate with Crauste before striking him with a clenched fist.

9. The France-Scotland match in Paris ended in a riot with home fans determined to let their feelings about the referee Mr Baxter be known after France were beaten 21-3. The home crowd had been riled by his fastidious attention to the detail of the laws of the game and were annoyed by decisions which, they felt, had cost their side the match. Only the quick-thinking of French wing Pierre Failliot, who smuggled the referee away to a taxi behind the stands straight after the final whistle, averted a lynching for Baxter. In a sad sequel to events, the Scottish Rugby Union decided to suspend its fixtures with France and the countries did not meet again until 1920.

10. Instead of trudging off in disgrace, the wily William McKenzie feigned a limp and hobbled off in front of 20,000 spectators who, under the impression that he was retiring through injury, gave him a warm round of applause. 'Offside' McKenzie was a pioneer of wing-forward play in New Zealand and his shady tactics in Sydney earned him the dubious honour of becoming the first man to be sent off while playing for New Zealand.

FAMOUS FOR 15 MINUTES

1. The New Zealander is the only sportsman who was capped in official rugby and cricket Tests AND refereed and umpired rugby and cricket Tests. He took charge of three rugby Tests: the first two involving the All Blacks and the British & Irish Lions in 1950, and the Dunedin international against Australia five years later. As a wicket-keeper and left-handed batsman he represented New Zealand in five consecutive Tests between 1937 and 1947, and later stood as an umpire in the first Test between New Zealand and England at Christchurch in 1959.

2. Not for nothing was Thomas known as 'Denzil drop' during his club days at Neath, before moving in the early 1950s to Llanelli where he impressed the 1953–54 touring All Blacks and came to the notice of the Welsh selectors. Equally at home as a centre or fly-half, in March 1954 he snatched victory from the jaws of a dull stalemate with a late dropped goal that made the final score 12-9 to Wales at Lansdowne Road, but was never chosen to represent his country again.

3. Owing to a translation misunderstanding, the club were mistaken for the famous Barbarians. On a visit to distribute toys to an orphanage they were met by an embassy official who thoughtfully arranged a match for them. When the day of their game arrived, they found themselves playing in the National Stadium against the host nation's crack club, Steaua Bucharest, in a match broadcast live on state television. Gladiators' lock, Nigel Jones, later admitted, 'We did our pre-match build up in the bar,' though the club's suspicions

had been aroused the night before when they were offered facilities for a training session. 'Not exactly our style,' added Jones.

4.   Both were capped for South Africa as wings against New Zealand. Stanley Osler played in a 17-0 win against the All Blacks at Durban in 1928, and Darius Botha was in the side that lost to the All Blacks at Christchurch in 1981. In addition, both made their single Test appearances in the company of their famous fly-half brothers. In 1928, Bennie Osler was in his prime as the Springboks' tactical controller and place-kicker, and Naas Botha was at fly-half for South Africa in 1981. Bennie and Naas went on to head the Springbok points-scoring charts of their day, and each captained the 'Boks.

5.   As his name suggests, Otto Nothling was of German descent. He was born in Queensland but won his rugby spurs during a long association with the Sydney University club while qualifying as a doctor. After his rugby career ended he was a noted Queensland cricketer and made his sole Test cricket appearance for Australia against England at the Sydney Cricket Ground in December 1928. He had an undistinguished match and never wore the baggy green in a Test again, but his unusual claim to fame is that he displaced arguably the greatest cricketer of all time for this match. Don Bradman had failed to make a mark in the opening Test of that series against England in Brisbane and, for the only time in his record-laden career, was dropped with Nothling taking his place.

6.   The QC Vernon Pugh, whose humble roots were in the mining community of the Amman Valley, was relatively inexperienced in the machinations of the International Board, rugby's ruling body, when he submitted for consideration a perceptive paper setting out the argument for embracing professionalism and ditching the game's defining stance on

amateurism. Summoning all his Gray's Inn barrister skills, he successfully steered his paper through the Board's Paris meeting in September 1995, *nem con* as the legal eagles have it. At one fell swoop, rugby was dragged into the 20th century, albeit 95 years late, but alas, the most inspired administrator rugby has known died young, struck down by cancer in his prime in April 2003.

7. Cigagna's long commitment as player and captain with Toulouse was finally rewarded by national recognition in 1995 when, aged 34, he was selected in the squad that travelled to South Africa for the third Rugby World Cup (RWC). France were knocked out in the semi-finals, earning them the right to a bronze-medal play-off against Will Carling's England. The French had not beaten *les rosbifs* for seven years but pulled off a 19-9 victory in Pretoria, the perfect end to Cigagna's first-class career. At the time he was the oldest man to make a Test debut for France and he remains the only player to gain an RWC medal in his sole international appearance.

8. Wing Alex Obolensky's Test debut in January 1936 was out of this world. The exiled Russian prince scored two tries on his Twickenham debut to send New Zealand to their first defeat on English soil. His second try was pure magic. He left a trail of defenders lying prostrate in his slipstream after a run that started on the right wing near halfway and finished wide out to the left of the posts. This try is regarded as one of the most memorable scores in Twickenham history, his feat earning him fame far beyond the proverbial 15 minutes. Although the 15 seconds of magic he showed against the All Blacks never again materialised in his brief, four-cap career, the intriguing backstory of how his family had rushed him over to England at the time of the Russian Revolution, together with his early death in a flying accident at the start of the Second World War, have helped his fame to endure.

9. He scored a hat-trick of tries on his Test debut, helping France to a 70-12 win against Zimbabwe in a pool match at Eden Park, Auckland, and was never again called on to represent his country – a unique achievement for a French one-cap wonder.

10. In a literal cock-up the reactionaries of the English selection panel managed to send out the match invitation to Alcock, a Guy's Hospital medical student of no especial rugby reputation, instead of contacting Lancelot Slocock, the Lancashire forward whom they had intended to select. Legend has it that when Alcock turned up for the match against South Africa at Crystal Palace in December 1906 a selector asked him who he was, and it was only then that the error came to light. Alcock nevertheless played and was awarded his cap, but he was never asked to wear the red rose of England again. Slocock gained his rightful place in England's pack for the 1907 International Championship matches, held it for two seasons, and skippered his country in 1908.

SHAKESPEAREAN CHARACTERS

1. Paul Sampson and Guy Gregory featured in the Wasps back divisions in the 1990s. Both gained representative honours, Sampson winning three caps as a fast-running wing between 1998 and 2001, while fly-half Gregory earned recognition at Student and Under-21 level, and also played for Emerging England.

2. The play is *Hamlet* and George Hamlet was the noted Irish forward who led his country's championship-title bid in 1911. He was a popular captain who took his men to the brink of a Triple Crown, losing only in a winner-takes-all showdown with Wales at Cardiff in March. All told he made 30 Test appearances for Ireland between 1902 and 1911 and was his country's leading cap-winner until the 1920s.

3. (Peter) Cranmer was a noted centre and mainstay of the England back division between 1934 and 1938. He captained England against Wales and Ireland in 1938. In Dublin, he led the red rose to an astonishing 36-14 win – unusually high scoring for the time – but was then inexplicably relieved of the captaincy for the final match of the season, against Scotland. He was also a gifted cricketer who played for and captained Warwickshire in the County Championship, and later wrote stylishly on both sports for *The Sunday Times*.

4. Orlando is the University of Life-educated male lead whose magnetic personality proves an irresistible force in the play, and Matías Orlando is the Pumas international whose forceful running made him an automatic choice in the national three-

quarter line. He won his first cap against Uruguay in 2012 but eventually became a fixture at outside centre in the sides managed by Daniel Hourcade in 2017 and 2018.

5. King John was the eponymous troublesome lead of the historical play and the name given to Barry John, the Welsh No. 10 who famously tormented the All Blacks in 1971, when the Lions won their only series to date in the land of the long white cloud. His ability to land his tactical kicks on a sixpence and slot goals with his no-nonsense style of kicking had the New Zealanders on the rack for the greater part of the four-Test rubber. Like Shakespeare's wicked king, he used all his powers to ruthlessly manipulate and ultimately exploit his opponents.

6. Travers is the Earl's servant; George and Bill Travers were the third of the small band of fathers and sons capped by Wales. George was Wales's earliest specialist hooker, winning 25 caps between 1903 and 1911, when there were fewer opportunities to make international appearances. His happiest playing hour was in Wales's 3-0 defeat of New Zealand in 1905 – the only time the Original All Blacks were beaten. His son Bill 'Bunner' Travers donned the hooker's shin pads for Wales a dozen times between 1937 and 1949, one of the select few to win caps before and after the Second World War. He also toured South Africa with the 1938 Lions.

7. Christened Macbeth, Duncan can claim to be the only rugby internationalist named after the Scottish play. His sole Test rugby appearance was an ominous tale for Scotland because it was their first defeat by Wales. Moreover, it was his opposite wing Tom Pryce-Jenkins who raced in for the only score of the match.

8. Bertram is the count. David Minto Bertram was a goal-kicking hooker who won 11 caps for Scotland between 1922 and 1924.

9. Argentina – Alonso and Miranda are the characters here. Martin Alonso was the Pumas full-back on their first tour to Britain in 1973 and played in five Tests during the 1970s, and the brothers Juan and Nicolás Fernández Miranda collectively played 75 times for Argentina between 1994 and 2007, as fly-half and scrum-half respectively.

10. Josh Valentine was the long-serving understudy to George Gregan and Luke Burgess for the Wallabies while the Valentine brothers, Dave (capped in 1947) and Alec (1953), were two of the legion of internationalists from that Scottish Borders rugby stronghold Hawick. Few remember Lancastrian Jim Valentine (capped 1890–96) now, but in his day he was regarded as one of the best wings ever to play for England. He was lost to the Union game in 1896 when his club Swinton joined the Northern Union (later known as the Rugby League). He was struck by lightning and killed instantly while on holiday with his wife in Barmouth in 1904.

CAPTAIN'S LOG

1.   The former Australian coach, never unwilling to throw the odd cat among the pigeons, named co-captains in Chris Robshaw and George Ford. It was the first time such a move had been made in a cap match, though Eddie had given the same pair the joint role for England's non-cap run-out against the Barbarians earlier in the year.

2.   Will Carling was only 22 when he began his England captaincy with a landmark victory over the Wallabies; he remained in charge throughout Cooke's stewardship as manager (1988–94) and two years beyond. The young Durham University graduate became the youngest man to lead the national side since Peter Howard had held the reins against Ireland in 1931, and he went on to set an all-time England record, leading them in 59 Tests.

3.   Seddon was drowned in an accident while sculling on the River Hunter in Maitland days before the match took place. In what must be a unique mark of respect to a captain, the photo – the most poignant in rugby's scrapbook – shows a vacant chair at its central focal point, a rugby ball marking the spot where Seddon's feet should have been.

4.   It was, admittedly, a long time ago, but when Wales won their first Grand Slam in 1908 they transferred the captain's armband around like a game of pass-the-parcel. For the opening game, Arthur 'Boxer' Harding of London Welsh led them to a 28-18 win against England at Bristol before the honour went to another forward, George Travers of Pill

Harriers, for the 6-5 triumph over Scotland at Swansea. Then, in a further demonstration of democracy, the selectors passed the captaincy to backs for the remaining two matches. Teddy Morgan, a wing, skippered them to a 36-4 win against France and full-back Bert Winfield was in charge when the Grand Slam was secured with an 11-5 defeat of Ireland in Belfast. A Grand Slam with a different captain in each round has never been repeated.

5. Clive Rowlands was a surprise choice when named to lead Wales on his Test debut against England at Cardiff in 1963. He retained the job for 14 successive caps – his entire international career – and enjoyed his finest hour in 1965 when he led the Principality to the Five Nations title and its first Triple Crown for 13 years. His omission from the Welsh team for the 1966 Five Nations was as big a bombshell as his original selection had been.

6. They both had the strength of character to omit themselves from Test sides when they felt unable to justify selection and handed the captaincy over to deputies. In New Zealand in 1966, Campbell-Lamerton ceded his duties on the field to Welsh outside-half David Watkins for the second and final Tests of the four-match series. In Britain and Ireland later that year, John Thornett caught impetigo early in the tour and was forced to stand down from playing for a few games. When he recovered his fitness, he felt that his form was not good enough to warrant selection for the Tests against Wales, Scotland, England and Ireland, and the reins were handed over to his vice-captain, Ken Catchpole.

7. Hornby and Stoddart are the only England rugby captains who also led their country at Test cricket. It was a long time ago. Hornby was England's boss twice on the rugby field in 1882 and was in command at The Oval later the same year when Australia won the famous Test match that gave rise to cricket's 'Ashes'. Stoddart captained England at both games

in 1893 and succeeded W.G. Grace leading England's 1894–95 Ashes mission to Australia.

8. Unusually all four were specialist scrum-halves, making it impossible for the captains and deputies to feature together in the run-on XVs for the Tests. De Villiers and Smith shared the leadership duties down under in 1965, playing three Tests apiece. Astre led France in both Tests in South Africa in 1975.

9. Domenech apparently flung the ball to his captain with an invitation to see what he could do with it. Prat promptly dropped a goal – one of two he landed that day to help France to a 16-11 victory.

10. Theo Pienaar, a front-row forward, did not appear in any of the Tests. He made eight appearances in New Zealand but transferred the captain's armband for the three-Test series to his tour vice-captain, 'Boy' Morkel. At 32, Pienaar was considered past his best as a forward, but his leadership skills off the field and his diplomacy at official functions made him the ideal candidate to lead the playing party.

LONDON CALLING

1. The Oval, HQ of the Surrey County Cricket Club, staged England's first home rugby Test and was the venue for all seven of England's home fixtures in the 1870s. It was a happy hunting ground: the men in white were never beaten there. Their maiden Test rugby win was recorded at The Oval when Scotland first ventured south in 1872, and England's overall record at the ground was six wins and a draw before matches were taken elsewhere in the early 1880s.

2. Wray took Saracens from its cosy London roots to Watford's Vicarage Road in south-west Hertfordshire. For years the town had been a rugby wilderness, better known in sporting circles for its football club, but Saracens, bankrolled by Nigel Wray, became the success story of professional rugby union's early days. On the field the club emerged as a class act thanks to some high-profile signings, and off it the creative marketing inspired by the dynamic Peter Deakin attracted new-found supporters like iron filings to a magnet. The upshot was that Watford was transformed from one of rugby union's black holes into one of its thriving hubs.

3. This was the nickname given to the Twickenham rugby ground in its early years. The ground was purchased by the Rugby Football Union (RFU) in 1907 for the princely sum of £5,573 and opened two seasons later. The playing area and surrounds were originally part of an orchard and market garden, and Billy Williams was the name of the RFU committee member who first identified the site's potential.

4. The RFU have staged only one home cap match in the capital since Twickenham opened. That was at Wembley in 1992 against Canada while Twickenham was undergoing refurbishment. England won that match 26-13, so can claim a 100 per cent winning record at the ground. They did play a Services international there against Scotland in 1942 (losing 8-5), and of course memorably lost 32-31 to Wales at Wembley in the last ever Five Nations match in 1999, but that counted as a 'home' game for the Welsh, whose stadium at Cardiff was then under reconstruction.

5. The Princess of Wales pub in Blackheath, which dates back to the early 1800s, was the headquarters for the Welsh team when they made their Test rugby bow against England across the common, at Mr Richardson's Field on 19 February 1881. Both teams changed there before England inflicted an overwhelming seven goals, six tries and a dropped goal to nil defeat on their visitors. Richardson's ground was sold to a property developer shortly after and the Blackheath club moved to a new base at Rectory Field on the Charlton Road a year or so later.

6. London's White City was the venue for the 1908 Olympic rugby union final. The full 15-a-side version of the game was an Olympic event at the 1900, 1908, 1920 and 1924 Games, though none of the four home unions, nor South Africa or New Zealand, ever entered a full team. The 1908 final was between Australia and 'Great Britain' who were represented by Cornwall, England's reigning county champions. The Wallabies, who were on their first tour of Britain, won the gold medal with a convincing 32-3 win. The sport was dropped after the 1924 Olympics but rugby has been revived for recent Games in its shorter, seven-a-side form.

7. Queen's in West Kensington. The club was originally established in 1886 as a multi-purpose sports complex and named after its patron, Queen Victoria. The facilities were

first-class and the billiard table-smooth playing surface was hailed as one of the best in the land for outdoor games. No wonder, then, that within a year of its establishment it became home to the Varsity match. Oxford and Cambridge played the first of 29 successive Varsity rugby matches at Queen's on 14 December 1887, when Cambridge, led by the splendidly named Scot Macbeth Duncan, won by a dropped goal and two unconverted tries to nil. In a close series, Oxford triumphed by 13 wins to 11 overall, with an abnormally high number of draws (five) before the fixture transferred in 1921 to Twickenham where it has remained ever since.

8. London fog. Not even the vast expertise of the Queen's Club ground staff could overcome the thick peasoupers that London, and West Kensington in particular, were prone to in the late 19th century; the one that occurred on 10 December 1890 was one of London's worst. The appointed morning of the match dawned dark and dreary with the ground enveloped in smog. The teams, having travelled down the previous day, agreed to a postponement, and the game had to be deferred twice more owing to fog before the Blues eventually fulfilled their fixture on 3 March 1891 – almost three months after the original date set for their clash.

9. The London Counties defeated Hennie Muller's Springboks 11-9 at Twickenham – the only defeat the touring South Africans suffered on an extended visit to Britain, Ireland and France. The tourists were regarded as the unofficial world champions, having blanked the All Blacks (4-0) in their most recent Test series, and their clean sweep through Britain in the first nine matches of their tour suggested that the tag was well deserved. But the well-prepared London Counties outfit ended their unbeaten record through a late penalty goal kicked by Alan Grimsdell, a timber engineer from Hertfordshire who inherited his talent for kicking footballs from his famous father Arthur, an FA Cup winner with Tottenham Hotspur in 1921 and former England football captain.

10. Wasps, formerly London Wasps, one of London's oldest clubs, tracing its foundation back to 1867. The club relocated to Coventry in December 2014, having enjoyed a rather nomadic London existence. They settled at Repton Avenue in Sudbury in the early 1920s and were a homely presence in north-west London until the end of the amateur era in 1995, at which point the club transferred its professional activities to Loftus Road in Shepherd's Bush. There followed a dozen years in Buckinghamshire playing at Adams Park in High Wycombe before the move to Coventry.

CONNECT THREE

1. Each enjoyed second international careers with another major Test-playing country. Dr Marsh was a Lancastrian who turned out for Scotland during his medical studies at Edinburgh University before returning to practise as a GP in his native Swinton. He was subsequently summoned by the English selectors to appear against Ireland in 1892 and holds the unique distinction of playing in the International Championship for two countries. Des Connor won a dozen caps for the Wallabies in the late 1950s before taking up a teaching appointment in Auckland and adding another dozen Test caps, this time of a black hue, to his Test collection. Shane Howarth was recruited by Graham Henry when he picked up the coaching reins of the Welsh national side in 1998. Howarth had been capped four times by New Zealand in 1994 and was ever-present for the first 19 matches of Henry's stewardship of Wales. He lost his place in the Welsh side in 2000 when his belief that his grandfather was Welsh-born could not be substantiated.

2. They are all known as the All Blacks. New Zealand requires no further explanation, but Neyland is a small village club in West Wales whose players even once wore the silver fern of their most famous namesakes. One legend has it that Neath adopted the all-black uniform when mourning the loss of a player named Dick Gordon, who died after sustaining a serious injury during a club match against Bridgend.

3. Public houses have been named after them. *The Stokes and Moncreiff*, named after the England and Scotland captains

in rugby's first international match, in 1871, opened near Twickenham a few years ago. The management certainly did its background research because the "'i" before "e" except in Moncreiff' is dead accurate in this case. Harry Watkins, a forward who featured in Wales's 1905 Triple Crown side, was a native of Carmarthenshire and became a pillar of the local community as a long-serving county alderman. He also dabbled with brewing – the inspiration, perhaps, for the name and hanging sign that bears his portrait at a hostelry in Felinfoel near Llanelli.

4. The three centre three-quarters had the unusual distinction of playing in the Five Nations Championship while studying in Britain, as well as appearing for southern hemisphere countries in Test cricket. Martin Donnelly was an outstanding batsman who played seven Test matches for New Zealand; Van Ryneveld (19 times) and Elgie (three) won Springbok cricket honours.

5. They captained winning teams for and against New Zealand. Jim Tilyard, who led Wellington to a 19-14 victory against the All Blacks in 1914, was the national skipper on their unbeaten tour of Australia in 1920. Cliff Porter skippered New Zealand 37 times between 1924 and 1930, including the famous Invincibles who blazed an unstoppable path through Europe and North America in 1924–25. After returning from that tour he led his province, Wellington, to a 10-6 win against Jim Donald's All Blacks on the eve of a tour to Australia in 1925 (for which Porter and members of his Invincibles were rested). Colin Meads, the greatest All Black of all time, first led New Zealand in a 9-3 win against a Transvaal Selection in 1960. In August 1973, near the end of his distinguished career, he led a NZRFU President's XV to a 35-28 win over the All Blacks in Wellington.

6. There's a clue hidden behind Davies and Grimmond's initials here. Howard Davies's first given name was Christmas and

Grimmond's second was Noel. The triad share Christmas Day birthdays.

7. Their parents were perhaps inspired by the legendary Welsh full-back J.P.R. Williams because they gave their offspring the great man's initials. And like the original J.P.R., Joseph Paul Richard Worsley, Jason Phillip Randall White and Jon-Paul Roger Pietersen enjoyed lengthy careers, winning more than 50 Test caps.

8. The three were noted pilots in their lives beyond the rugby field. The fabled Prince Obolensky joined the RAF shortly before the outbreak of the Second World War and was serving as a Pilot Officer when he was killed in a flying accident at Martlesham Heath Airfield in March 1940. Rory Underwood, an officer with the RAF throughout his long England and Lions Test career, was as ferociously fast on the field as the jet fighters he flew, while younger brother Tony, similarly blessed with natural speed, followed the commercial route, piloting long-haul for Virgin Atlantic before taking the controls of the Airbus 380 for Emirates.

9. They were the first three players to achieve the double of Super Rugby and European Champion honours with their clubs.

PLAYER	SUPER FINAL WINNER	EUROPEAN CHAMPION
Rod Kafer	2001 with the Brumbies	2002 with Leicester
Doug Howlett	2003 with the Blues	2008 with Munster
Brad Thorn	2008 with the Crusaders	2012 with Leinster

Thorn, moreover, played international rugby for New Zealand in two Tri-Nations Grand Slam-winning teams (in 2003 and 2010), in another Tri-Nations title-win in 2008 and was a member of their Rugby World Cup-winning team in 2011, entitling him to claim that he has been rugby union's most successful player of the professional era.

10. The trio are best known as first-class players who became international referees, a rare achievement in post-war rugby (though more common before 1939). Bob McMullen was a New Zealand Test player in the 1950s and later refereed at international level. Ireland's Alain Rolland, a fluent French-speaker, was also an international and Test referee, while Glen Jackson is one of the current New Zealand officials on the list of elite international referees. His first-class playing career included stints in Super Rugby with The Chiefs and six years in England as a fly-half for Saracens.

ORIGINS OF THE GAME

1. William Webb Ellis is the name on the plaque. He left the school in 1825 and went up to Oxford, where he won a Cricket Blue in the first recognised university match of its kind. But the story is now regarded as rugby's biggest conspiracy theory – a mix of half-truths and fake news concocted by the Old Rugbeian Society in its 1897 pamphlet on the origins of the game. Significantly, none of rugby's early histories mentions Ellis by name, though that didn't deter the Home Unions from celebrating the sport's 'centenary' by staging a four-countries match between England and Wales, and Scotland and Ireland on The Close at Rugby School in 1923. Moreover, the fact that the Ellis myth has been largely debunked by historians hasn't bothered World Rugby, the game's governing body, whose showcase Rugby World Cup is played for the Webb Ellis Cup.

2. New Zealand. The land of the long white cloud dates the beginning of its devotion to rugby to 1870, when young Charles John Monro, recently returned from the rugby-playing school in London, persuaded local youths in Nelson to take part in a game under Rugby rules. In 1947, Arthur Swan, the official historian of New Zealand Rugby Football Union, defined the meeting of The College and The Town at the Nelson Botanical Reserve on 14 May 1870, as the first inter-club rugby match staged in New Zealand.

3. The match was between McGill University of Montreal and Harvard, and took place in Cambridge, Massachusetts. It set the rugby ball rolling in the USA, but the students who

were so keen to take up the pastime adapted the rules so extensively that by 1880 the game had evolved into gridiron, which to this day is regarded as America's main football code.

4. The exhibition game was staged in Turin and sparked off interest in Italy. A Frenchman residing in Milan was instrumental in raising the first Italian club side, captaining a local team that was beaten 15-0 by a visiting French Selection the year later. Rugby, however, was suspended in Italy during the Great War and did not resume until the mid-1920s, when Piero Mariani, after a brief exile in France, pioneered the game in a number of locations. The national union was formed soon after, a thriving club championship was established and Italy played their first international match in 1929. The *Azzurri* became the sixth nation of the annual International Championship in 2000.

5. British railway engineers surveying and overseeing the building of Argentina's national railway network established rugby as their principal game, organising matches in Buenos Aires as a suitable sporting diversion between cricket seasons. By 1890, there were a dozen clubs thriving in the capital and the Argentine Rugby Union was founded in 1899.

6. Prior to the goodwill shown by the New Zealand Rugby Football Union, the Islanders used coconut shells, which must have made kicking the 'ball' quite hazardous.

7. Ireland and Australia can point to two of the longest-established rugby clubs still in existence. Trinity undergraduates from Rugby School are believed to have played their *alma mater*'s brand of football in Dublin's College Park before 1855, when R.H. Scott, another Old Rugbeian, placed an advertisement in a Dublin newspaper announcing a match between original and new members of the Dublin University Football Club. In Australia, the Sydney University Club began in 1863 and, like their Dublin counterparts, are still going strong.

8. It was the men of the 1890 Pioneer Column raised in the Cape by Cecil Rhodes who, on their weary trek north to Salisbury, offered Zimbabwe (formerly Rhodesia) its first glimpse of rugby. They and the troopers that followed them established clubs in Bulawayo and Salisbury, and in 1895 the Rhodesia Rugby Union was formed.

9. Although there is pictorial evidence to suggest that rugby was played in Japan as early as 1874, the country's first club was founded by Tanaka when he resumed his studies at Keio University. In 1900, their first matches were played against British enthusiasts resident in Yokohama, and by 1911 several university and school clubs were engaging in annual tournaments.

10. Wales. *The Fighting Parsons* was the appropriate title of Selwyn Walters's engrossing tale about rugby at St David's College, Lampeter, an educational institution renowned for its theology. The college boys played the first recorded rugby match in the Principality when they met Llandovery College in 1866.

UNEXPECTED INTERRUPTIONS

1. The Lions were halfway through their tour when they met Wanganui at Spriggens Park. The scores were level when referee Sam Lemon awarded the Lions a penalty, which Bev Risman prepared to plant between the poles. His kicking preliminaries, however, met with uproar from the 20,000 capacity crowd because the ball had earlier gone into touch without the referee noticing. The locals were baying for blood when, amid the commotion, a burly bobby whose understanding of rugby's laws matched his knowledge of those enforced in his daily duties tipped off Mr Lemon that the Wanganui touch judge's flag remained raised. The referee allowed the kick to go ahead, but after Risman had steered the ball through the posts he consulted his touch judge and scrubbed the score, bringing the game back to the touchline and awarding a throw-in instead. The match ended with the Lions happy to eke out a 9-6 win.

2. Cardiff Arms Park was so wet and muddy that, after an hour in the quagmire conditions, the teams had become so mud-spattered it was impossible to tell them apart. So, on the hour, the canny Mr Taylor ordered the entire Welsh XV off the field to the sheds for a swift change of kit. The change worked wonders for Wales: ten minutes after their return their full-back, Terry Davies, lifted the heavy ball out of the morass to give his side the winning lead with a penalty from point-blank range. The next season the International Board introduced a new law prohibiting teams leaving the field during a match.

3. Jim Lenehan and Terry Curley of the Wallabies and Fenwick Allison and George Cole of the Counties combination were four of the most prodigious out-of-the-hand kickers in rugby in the late 1950s. During the course of an otherwise forgettable match they managed to land three balls high onto the Highfield Road grandstand's roof. When Allison planted the third ball out of reach, play ground to a complete halt. This being a football ground, there were no spares or practice balls available. The only option was for the ground staff to find long ladders and clamber onto the roof to recover the lost rugby balls, much to the relief of the 10,000 spectators present.

4. The curious incident of the man and the dog in the second match between Oxford and Cambridge occurred when the hound bit the Oxford forward George Podmore, causing a long break in play while he received attention.

5. London Irish, in front of a record home crowd, were only a point behind favourites Leicester when, five minutes into the second half, a call went out over the PA system for the owner of a green Volvo to please remove his car immediately as it was obstructing essential safety access. As a scrum was about to set, Gary Halpin, the Exiles skipper and tight-head, held the front rows up as the message sank in. The registration number of the Volvo matched his! Play was suspended while he rumbled back to the changing rooms to find his car keys so that the offending vehicle could be shifted. His side never recovered after that and Leicester accelerated away to a 46-21 win that landed them an RFU Cup Final showdown with Bath.

6. The 1991 match at Colorado Springs started in a downpour, but when thunder and lightning struck perilously close to the ground the referee, Albert Adams of South Africa, abandoned the match at half-time, citing safety reasons.

7. The British and Irish Cup tie at Aberavon's Talbot Athletic ground was at an exciting stage when a sink-hole caused by a leaking drainpipe suddenly opened up on the playing surface. Aberavon officials quickly tried to repair the damage but Bristol refused to continue for health and safety reasons. The Cup committee reviewed the incident and ruled that there should be a replay. The rematch was staged incident-free a couple of months later, this time resulting in a clear-cut win for the English club.

8. Play was interrupted early on when the stadium's sprinkler system was suddenly activated from its underground emplacements and gave the players an unexpected hose-down. As it was a very hot afternoon, they viewed the intrusion as a welcome refreshing break, but Rugby World Cup organisers who had booked the ground to stage several matches in its showpiece event barely a month later were far from impressed.

9. South Africa were playing old rivals New Zealand at Kings Park when a spectator from Potchefstroom ran on to the field early in the second half and bizarrely tackled Irish referee David McHugh, who dislocated his shoulder. A long hold-up ensued while the official was replaced and the idiotic intruder was restrained and escorted from the ground. England's Chris White, one of the touch judges, controlled the last 30 minutes of the game and the spectator was charged with assault and handed a lifetime ban from watching South African rugby matches.

10. The Springboks tour of New Zealand in 1981 took place against the constant backdrop of anti-apartheid demonstrations. Barbed wire and police batons featured as frequently as rugby balls in photographic coverage of the tour. The visitors were kept under close security throughout their six-week stay and two of the planned matches were

actually cancelled before the drama reached a climax in Auckland during the final Test of the three-match series. A Cessna aircraft strafed the Eden Park ground with flares and leaflets, and even flour-bombed the players, on one occasion temporarily stunning the All Black prop Gary Knight. Despite Mr Norling's offer to call the match off, both captains insisted that the Test should run its course and the ultimate moment of drama arrived in the final minutes when New Zealand's full-back, Allan Hewson, landed the deciding penalty (25-22) and settled the series (2-1).

NICKNAMES

1. 'The Blackpool Tower' was the alias of Wade Dooley, the community policeman whose big, powerful presence in the second row revitalised the 1989 Lions and was a reliable source of gilt-edged possession for the England sides who won back-to-back Grand Slams in 1991 and 1992. In his day he was the tallest player in the British game, but the most remarkable fact about his career in the dying days of amateur rugby was that he proved that an Englishman could still make the grade at the top level despite playing for an unfashionable club. For most of a long England career his elongated frame was to be found in the ranks of Preston Grasshoppers, two levels below the top echelons of the English club structure.

2. Ian Smith was the original 'Flying Scotsman', named after the steam engine built in 1923 to create record times for the London to Edinburgh express route. Smith began his Test career in 1924 and in 32 appearances for Scotland until 1933 ran in a staggering 24 tries – a world Test record that stood until David Campese's days in the limelight more than 60 years later.

3. 'The Bayonne Express' was the nickname in his playing day of Patrice Lagisquet, the man from Arcachon who once clocked 10.8 seconds for the 100 metres. That blistering pace brought him 20 tries on the rugby field for France in 46 Tests between 1983 and 1991. After a coaching stint with Biarritz, he joined the national coaching team as assistant to Philippe Saint-André after the 2011 Rugby World Cup.

4. It was the dark humour of a team-mate that bestowed the moniker 'The Cambridge Milk-float' on Mark Bailey. Before becoming High Master of St Paul's School and Professor of Later Medieval History at the University of East Anglia, Bailey was a gifted sportsman who won seven caps for England between 1984 and 1990, but even his best friends would agree that pace was not his greatest asset. At the time of the 1990 French match he was an academic at Cambridge University, where he had earlier gained four Blues, two as captain.

5. He was Lt-Col. J.E.C. Partridge to the Newport faithful at Rodney Parade in later life, but he was 'Birdy' to the South Africans who took the field for the opening Test of the 1903 series against the touring British/Irish team. He had captured the selectors' attention playing for Pretoria Harlequins while serving as a young officer with the Welch Regiment in South Africa and was pitched into a pack that held the tourists to a nil-all draw in Johannesburg. When the duties of service life permitted, he turned out for Newport and later Blackheath between 1898 and 1911, and while stationed near Gravesend in 1906 actually played for Kent against the first South African side to tour Britain – Paul Roos's original Springboks.

6. Dai Morris, capped 34 times in the Welsh back row between 1967 and 1974, was 'The Shadow'. His career coincided with the first half of Gareth Edwards's reign as scrum-half, a purple patch for Wales that included a Grand Slam, two Triple Crown wins and almost complete dominance of the Five Nations. Morris was Edwards's 'minder' in the side, a quiet presence who was never more than a pace away supporting the great man – always there in the scrum-half's shadow.

7. Gould was to Welsh rugby what Dr W.G. Grace was to English cricket – a household name, but it was for his agility climbing trees as a youngster that he was christened 'Monkey' or 'Monk'. It was a skill that never left him and was put to good use on the occasion of the 1887 Wales-England international

at Llanelli's Stradey Park. Snow and ice had frozen the ground, so arrangements were hastily made to erect impromptu goals and stage the game on the adjoining cricket pitch. A little too hastily, perhaps, for during the course of the match one of the crossbars was dislodged and eventually collapsed, whereupon the sprightly Gould lived up to his moniker, nonchalantly shinning up the posts and quickly replacing the fallen bar.

8. Ian McLauchlan was the Lions loose-head and man of the match who delivered the British/Irish combination a 9-3 win against New Zealand in Dunedin to put the tourists one up in the series. Beforehand the sceptics had suggested that he was too small to be effective against the All Blacks, but the 5ft 8½in Scot burrowed underneath his much-vaunted opponent to completely disrupt the New Zealand pack, and his try from a charge-down just before half-time proved to be the decisive score of an edgy Test. When he walked off the pitch, Lions manager Dr Doug Smith greeted him with the words: 'You are some Mighty Mouse,' ... and 'Mighty Mouse' he has been ever since to rugby folk worldwide.

9. John Eales was nicknamed 'Nobody' because, his colleagues argued, whether jumping in the line-out, handling in open play or even kicking important goals under pressure, 'nobody's perfect'.

10. 'Monsieur Drop' was Pierre Albaladejo, who staggered sports followers in April 1960 when he became the first player to land three dropped goals in a major international match. He'd won a couple of caps as a full-back six years earlier, but installed in his natural position for the first time in 1960, he fired France to a share of the Five Nations title by landing dropped goals off both feet in France's 23-6 demolition of Ireland at the old Stade Colombes ground in Paris. France played champagne rugby that day, and did so for most of Albaladejo's champagne career up to 1965, when he retired with a dozen dropped goals to his credit – a then Test record.

MORE NAME GAMES

1. Charlie Jordan's second given name was Garibaldi, after the Italian nationalist who was in his prime in 1859 when Jordan first saw the light of day. His parents must have been uncertain or in disagreement about how to name their young child, because the birth was registered at Newport as plain 'Male' Jordan. He was a regular in the Newport packs of the 1880s and was in his prime when, in 1884, he was press-ganged into making up Ireland's numbers when they arrived at Cardiff with only 13 fit men. Jordan later lived in England and died in Newcastle upon Tyne on 20 October 1912, aged 52.

2. Kingstone was named after Napoleon. Referred to during his rugby career as 'Nap', he played throughout the inaugural Test series between New Zealand and South Africa in 1921. Time and again Kingstone saved the All Blacks with brave defence in the final Test of that series, a scoreless draw that tied the rubber at a win apiece with one result shared. Serious injuries sustained in a car accident 12 months later forced him into premature retirement from the game.

3. Terry Holmes was the lion-hearted Cardiff scrum-half who relished taking on the 'All Whites' lock Richard Moriarty in the 1980s when leading Welsh clubs took each other on four times a season. They formed a formidable combination when they joined forces nine times in the national cause between 1981 and 1985.

4. His full birth name was registered as Saint David Cyril James Joynson by his parents, but by the time his refereeing career

was in full swing in the mid-1950s he preferred to present himself as the more cosmopolitan David Cyril Joynson. Even so, he is the only 'patron saint' to referee a rugby Test, taking control of the 1955 Calcutta Cup match at Twickenham. As Cyril Joynson, he remained an unassuming and loyal servant to rugby in Monmouthshire for many years, writing an instructional rugby book for boys and refereeing schools matches until his sixties.

5.   Everyone knows of the ubiquitous A.N. Other, but A. Forward – Allen Forward of Pontypool – was the name of a Pontypool forward who won half a dozen caps as a flanker in 1951 and 1952 when Wales won the Five Nations Grand Slam.

6.   The composers were Haydn and Handel, which were uncommon names in the UK until the early years of the 20th century, and the two players were Haydn Tanner (Swansea and Cardiff) and Handel Greville (Llanelli). Tanner was first capped as a teenager in Wales's 13-12 defeat of the All Blacks in 1935, and but for the war he would almost certainly have become the first player to win 50 caps. Between 1935 and 1949, Tanner was restricted to only 25 caps as Wales's first choice half-back because there were no Tests between 1939 and 1947. In the event, he missed only one official international – against Australia in December 1947 – when an injured elbow forced him to withdraw on the eve of the match. That's when Greville stepped up to win his sole cap in his place and played a blinder in a 6-0 victory at Cardiff, but never again had the opportunity to represent the Principality.

7.   There were plenty of famous All Blacks to choose from among the 1963–64 tourists: Colin Meads, Don Clarke, Waka Nathan, Mac Herewini, Ken Gray and Wilson Whineray to name a few. But the player who most impressed the Irishman was another legend. He named his son Kelvin Tremain Leahy, after the dynamic All Black loose forward who went on to win 38 caps for New Zealand in a distinguished career that

spanned the years 1959–68. Mick Leahy was capped against Wales soon after the All Blacks departed, displacing the great Willie John McBride as a lock in the Irish XV. Leahy junior was born in 1965 and followed in his father's international footsteps in 1992, making his Ireland debut in their back row against New Zealand in Dunedin.

8. Kenneth James Forbes Scotland was the running full-back whose attacking play as the last line of defence placed him ten years ahead of his time on the 1959 Lions tour. At a time when full-backs were only expected to catch, tackle and kick for touch, Ken Scotland showed a rare flair for joining three-quarter line movements as the extra man, and had a penchant for try-scoring – something full-backs rarely did in his day. He was such a versatile player in fact, that he turned out as a scrum-half, stand-off and centre, as well as at full-back on that Lions tour, and was also a useful round-the-corner place-kicker.

9. His full name was Edward Verdun Watkins and he was born during the second week of the famous battle on the Western Front. Making his debut in Wales's 13-12 win against the All Blacks in 1935, Eddie Watkins won eight caps before joining Wigan Rugby League club in 1939.

10. Tucker was named as a replacement for the Irish side against France in Paris in 1980 but even he must have raised an eyebrow when he saw in the match programme that an 'F' had been used instead of a 'T' in his surname. It is easily rugby's most famous misprint. Then, when Tucker replaced John O'Driscoll early in the game, the unsuspecting French stadium announcer heralded his arrival by referring to the name given in the programme using 'that' word, much to the amusement of the Irish contingent present.

BRAINTEASERS

1. Anyone on good terms with the numbers between nought and one will appreciate that ⅝ is the fraction that falls between ½ and ¾. As rugby developed in Britain in the late 19th century, all backs were regarded as defenders. The half-backs – literally those halfway between the forwards and the full-back – played left and right, standing level with one another either side of their pack, but feeding scrums on their side of the field and standing off on the other side. The line of players between them and the full-back were, with absolute arithmetic rectitude, called three-quarters.

   In New Zealand, however, half-back play evolved differently, with one specialist half-back always working the scrum anywhere on the field, while the other stood back as a first receiver should his partner choose to feed the ball out. It became the custom for a second receiver to position himself next to the standing-off half, but ahead of the three-quarters. These two 'receivers' between the half-back and three-quarters became known as the five-eighths. Their equivalents in the British system of course are the fly-half (or outside- or stand-off half) and the inside centre, but the tradition in the Home Unions has been to retain the old-fashioned positional names.

2. Say the required Welsh leeway was x points. Their pre-match difference was 29 while England's was 43. So Wales needed a winning margin that satisfied the inequality:

   $$29 + x > 43 - x$$
   Then $2x > 14$
   So $x > 7$

On the day, the dragon roared in the second half and Wales accelerated to a sensational 30-3 victory that comfortably swung the title their way.

3. New Zealand enthusiasts will probably know the answers off the top of their heads: Dan Carter 1,598 points; Andrew Mehrtens 967 and Grant Fox 645. Others can work them out by simply adding the three statements together, halving and subtracting the original combinations.

   The addition result, 6,420, clearly represents *double* the total scored by the three players. So halving gives a total of 3,210 for Carter and Mehrtens and Fox altogether. Subtracting the three sums originally given in the question from 3,210 in turn yields:

Grant Fox:	$3,210 - 2,565 = 645$ points
Dan Carter:	$3,210 - 1,612 = 1,598$ points
Andrew Mehrtens:	$3,210 - 2,243 = 967$ points

4. Let the values of a try, conversion and penalty be x, y and z respectively and look for whole number solutions of the simultaneous equations:

   $$3x + y + z = 14$$
   $$4x + y = 14$$

   The solution is that tries (x) were valued at three points, conversions (y) two and penalty goals (z) three.

5. The revised simultaneous equations become …

   $$3x + y + z = 12$$
   $$4x + y = 11$$

   … for which the required solution now is that tries (x) were valued at only two points, conversions (y) three and penalty goals (z) three. The penalty kicked in the late stages by the

Welsh full-back Billy Bancroft was the winning score, and set Wales on the road to their first Triple Crown success.

6. For as long as the giver's hands are pointing sideways or backwards, then the pass is deemed legal – even when the subsequent track of the ball is forward. This guidance emanated from World Rugby, the game's ruling body, and represents one of their most enlightened judgements. For years spectators have yelled 'forward, referee' as passes have gone unpunished. The reality, however, is that for players and good officials keeping up with play, the only way to judge the trajectory of a pass is to view its motion *relative* to the speed of the passer. That's why the new guidance has been so appropriate: judging velocity is impossible when players are moving at pace. Consider, for example, a player running at 8mph parallel with a touchline and throwing the ball directly behind his head at 6mph to a backer-up. To the players and officials keeping up with the passer, this is clearly a pass back and under recent guidance must be regarded as legal, even though those seated in the stands or watching on television will see this as a pass with the ball travelling forward at a speed of 2mph.

7. Conversions must be attempted from anywhere on the line through the point of touchdown parallel with the touchline. If range, elevation and the conditions are to be neglected, this becomes a geometrical exercise in maximising the angle subtended by the goalposts with the kicker.

    Imagine a circle through the base of the two uprights but large enough to cut the line of the conversion. There will be two points, A and B, where the circle cuts the line. Since the base line between the posts is a chord of the circle, the angles subtended at A and B will be the same (because angles in the same segment are equal).

    Now consider smaller such circles for which the points A and B fall closer together. Clearly the angles subtended are greater than for the cases where A and B were wider apart. Eventually a circle will be found which just touches the line of the conversion (which in mathematical parlance is the tangent to the circle). This point of contact optimises the angle for the kicker.

8. At the time of the 1988 RFU Cup Final, Bristol were noted for using letters instead of numbers on their jerseys. H, I and J were the shirts worn by their front row of loose-head Austin Phillips, hooker Dave Palmer and tight-head John Doubleday, corresponding to jerseys numbered one, two and three worn by most other teams. Bristol's lettering began with full-back Jon Webb wearing letter A, so A = 15 is the required answer.

9. Each team plays four times so all told there were ten matches. The sole draw must have been France with Wales, since they were the only nations to finish with odd tournament points. Wales therefore won their other three games (against Scotland, Ireland and England). Since Ireland lost to Wales but finished with six points, they must have beaten France, England and Scotland; England must have beaten Scotland and France; and Scotland beat France.

Uniquely, these were the outcomes of the 1969 Five Nations matches. Wales won the Triple Crown that season, but could only draw (8-all) with France at Stade Colombes in Paris.

10. Wales (7 points) and France (1 point) would clearly have to draw only one match in this hypothetical case, though not necessarily when they played one other.

Obviously the maximum possible number of draws for any one of the other three countries is four, but would only fit England's outcome, implying that Wales beat Ireland. However, since Ireland would need to draw with England, there arises the contradiction that Ireland would finish with fewer than six championship points. So no country could draw all four of its matches. Clearly none of England, Scotland or Ireland could draw three matches because their points tally would be an odd number. So the final case to consider is if one or more of these three could draw twice.

Logic then shows an outcome consistent with the table if Wales beat England, Scotland and France but drew with Ireland; Ireland beat Scotland and France but also drew against England; England beat France but also drew with Scotland; and Scotland also drew with France.

So, all told, no more than four drawn matches can satisfy the final table.

(The most drawn games recorded in any Five Nations Championship season (1910–99) was three: in 1922, 1962, 1974 and 1979.)

TROPHY CABINET

1. The Bledisloe Cup is awarded to the winners of Test series between New Zealand and Australia. Named after the then Governor-General of New Zealand, it was originally won by the All Blacks in 1931 and was the first trophy assigned for a match or rubber between southern hemisphere Test nations.

2. James Bevan was born at St Kilda, Melbourne, Victoria, in 1858 but was orphaned as a child when his parents were lost at sea. His father's roots were in Grosmont and James was sent 'home' to the Welsh Marches, where he was educated at Hereford Cathedral School before going up to Cambridge University and winning rugby Blues in 1877 and 1880. In 1881, he was appointed captain of Wales for the Principality's inaugural cap match, against England at Blackheath. He was originally destined for the legal profession but switched career to become a clergyman, and lived most of his life in England where he sired seven sons, six of whom followed him into the church. The James Bevan Trophy was commissioned in 2007 by the commercial arm of the Welsh Assembly Government to mark the upcoming centenary of fixtures between the two nations that had had such close ties to Bevan's early years.

3. The year 1988 marked 1,000 years of Dublin city, and to mark the occasion the Irish Rugby Union invited England to play an additional cap match for the specially struck Millennium Trophy. The helmet-shaped gold and silver trophy on a black marble base was presented to England after beating the men in green 21-10 at Lansdowne Road in

April 1988, and the two sides have competed annually for the handsome sculpture ever since.

4.   The Cook Cup is named after the explorer of that name and the protagonists are England and Australia. It was launched in 1997, early in the professional era, when the Wallabies and the RFU agreed to stage annual fixtures.

5.   The trophy is contested between France and New Zealand and was first awarded to New Zealand on Armistice Day, 2000. Dave Gallaher was the revered skipper of the First All Blacks, who toured Europe and North America losing only once during their marathon 35-match visit in 1905–06. A decade later, as a respected sergeant, he served on the Western Front during the Great War, which claimed his life at Passchendaele in October 1917. When the famous All Blacks 'Invincibles' came to Europe in 1924–25, the tourists made a pilgrimage to his grave at Poperinghe Military Cemetery in Belgium and paid their respects by laying two wreaths, one by skipper Cliff Porter on behalf of the All Blacks and the other by Freddie Lucas, one of the tourists whose home club, Ponsonby, was also Gallaher's. That informal ceremony has become a part of All Blacks' tour programmes in France, making it entirely appropriate that the trophy should celebrate the longstanding ties between the nations.

6.   The Hillary Shield, honouring the famous Kiwi mountaineer who was the first to conquer Everest, is awarded to the winner of Test matches between England and New Zealand. The Shield, featuring Sir Edmund Hillary set against a Himalayan backdrop, was struck after his death in January 2008 and was first presented by his widow to Richie McCaw when the All Blacks beat England at Twickenham to complete a Grand Slam of the Home Unions later the same year. The All Blacks have held it the most times since.

7. Although their rich common rugby history is nearly a hundred years old (dating back to 1921), it is only since 2004 that New Zealand and South Africa's rivalry has been rewarded with a trophy: the Freedom Cup. It was introduced to mark the tenth anniversary of the political transition from the apartheid system to majority rule in South Africa.

8. The number 46664 is identified with the South African teams who have played Australia for the Nelson Mandela Challenge Plate introduced in 2000. For these matches the Springboks wear the number on their sleeves in memory of South Africa's first post-apartheid president Nelson Mandela, who for his political beliefs was the 466th inmate imprisoned on Robben Island in 1964 and consequently numbered prisoner 46664.

9. The Lansdowne Cup for Tests between Australia and Ireland was presented to the Australian Rugby Union by the Lansdowne club of Sydney. The attractive glass trophy is made of Waterford Crystal and was introduced in 1999 when Australia staged a two-Test series against the Irish.

10. Scotland is the common factor. They play for the Hopetoun Cup against Australia (first contested in 1998 and named after the Scot who was a Governor General of Australia), the Centenary Quaich against Ireland (first presented in 1989 when the old rivals met for the 100th time), and the Auld Alliance Trophy against France (launched in 2018 to honour the players of both countries who laid down their lives during the Great War).

THE NUMBERS GAME

1. Scoreless draws in Tests are rare nowadays. The last 0-0 result was in January 1964, when Scotland held Wilson Whineray's All Blacks at Murrayfield. There was a rash of pointless Tests in the early 1960s: France and South Africa in Paris in 1961; England and Wales at Twickenham in 1962; and Ireland and England in 1963 immediately preceded the Murrayfield draw.

2. The No. 8 position was the last one established in team formations. Early scrums were free-for-alls in which forwards tried to kick the ball through a melee of bodies. Gradually, heeling evolved as a method of gaining possession, and with it came the need for specialist hookers. Winging, packing loosely at the back of the scrum, was also in vogue by the early years of the 20th century, but specialisation was generally frowned upon; forwards were primarily selected on their all-round abilities. Scrums were formed on the first-up, first-down principle – that is, the first three to arrive were the players who made up the front row. The favoured formations were 3-2-3 or 3-3-2 because these enabled forwards to wheel the scrum and break away with the ball at their feet. Indeed, dribbling was considered as important a skill for forwards as shoving, tackling and passing. Then, between the wars, the Springboks began experimenting with the 3-4-1 formation, leaving just one man in the back row. This was the player they christened the 'eighthman'. The advantage of the South African system was that the scrum-half feeding the ball had more protection from his flankers than in the 3-2-3 arrangement, and the ball emerged much quicker from the scrum, giving backs that precious extra second when

launching attacks. The system gradually took hold elsewhere from the 1930s, though it was the All Blacks who shortened the term eighthman to No 8. By the early 1960s the position had become universally adopted, the Scots finally falling into line after adhering to the old 3-2-3 scrum for most of the preceding decade.

3.   The most painful memory for Scotland's rugby fans is their record streak of 17 Test defeats bookended by two famous wins against Wales at Murrayfield: 19-0 in February 1951 and 14-8 in 1955.

4.   The scoreline at Murrayfield on 6 February 1971, when Wales came from behind to win thanks to a late Gerald Davies try that was successfully converted by flanker John Taylor with 'the greatest conversion since St Paul's' according to former Scotland cap and man of wit Jim McPartlin. The 19-18 win was a match packed with twists and turns that saw the lead change hands six times. Wales went on to win the Grand Slam.

5.   The record winning streak by a Tier One nation is 18, set by New Zealand between August 2015 and October 2016, which included their 2015 Rugby World Cup triumph. The run ended in Chicago in November 2016, when a fired-up Ireland side ran up a remarkable 40-29 success over the world champions. The record was subsequently matched by England during the early part of Eddie Jones's reign as national team coach, and was also ended by Ireland (at the Aviva Stadium, Lansdowne Road, in 2017).

6.   It's hard to imagine, but this is the world record for the *fewest* spectators at a rugby international involving a Tier One nation. The match between United States and South Africa was staged at Owl Creek Polo Field in Glenville near Albany, New York, in September 1981. The explanation for the low turnout was that the venue was kept secret to avoid anti-apartheid demonstrations, and according to some sources the visitors

and hosts had to help clear the field of horse manure before the match could take place. The Springbok flanker Thys Burger created an unusual record in this Test. He was called on to help erect the posts for the Test, then acted as touch judge when the match kicked off, and eventually came on to win a cap as a substitute when Theuns Stofberg was injured early in the second half. South Africa won the game 38-7.

7. An easy one this for any self-respecting Welsh rugby historian. The figure represents the caps won for Wales – all consecutively – by Sir Gareth Edwards, if not the greatest Welshman of all time, almost certainly the Principality's greatest rugby player. He began his Test career as a teenager on April Fool's Day, 1967, against France in Paris and was an ever-present for 11 years, becoming the first Welsh player to reach 50 caps before winding up his career in the Grand Slam victory over France in Cardiff in March 1978.

8. The figure represents the current world record for most appearances in Tests and is held by New Zealand's Richie McCaw. His 148 Test appearances for the All Blacks between 2001 and 2015 include the unique distinction of leading two Rugby World Cup-winning sides: in 2011 and 2015.

9. Another New Zealand-held world Test record: the career points accumulated by Dan Carter, comprising 29 tries, 293 conversions, 281 penalties and eight dropped goals during his 112-cap reign as the All Blacks' playmaker and goal-kicker between 2003 and 2015. The list of previous record holders reads like a roll-call of the world's greatest rugby players, including Don Clarke, Phil Bennett, Andy Irvine, Grant Fox, Michael Lynagh, Neil Jenkins and Jonny Wilkinson.

10. This figure is the official world record attendance for a Test. It was set at Stadium Australia in Sydney for the 2000 Bledisloe Cup clash – 109,844 more than turned out for the USA-SA Test of 1981.

QUOTE, UNQUOTE

1. All Blacks skipper Andy Leslie made this dry comment after his side had swamped Scotland 24-0 at Auckland's Eden Park in June 1975. The match was played on a paddy field after teeming rain drowned New Zealand on the morning of the match, leaving vast areas of the ground under several inches of water and causing traffic havoc for those attending the match. Commercial incentives were the drivers behind staging the Test. Scotland were due to fly home the next day so there was no prospect of a postponement, while cancellation would have meant returning nearly £100k of advance ticket sales. So both sides agreed that the Test should go ahead. Scotland prop Sandy Carmichael, who equalled Hughie McLeod's national cap record that day by making his 40th appearance, reckoned he'd actually played in more difficult conditions, saying, 'I once played in four inches of snow, and that was worse. Mind, I was worried at Auckland because I can't swim very well.'

2. Easily the most successful of England's seven coaches before the Geoff Cooke era took off in the late 1980s was the Torquay redhead Mike Davis, who had served a long rugby apprenticeship, winning 16 caps in the red rose second row between 1963 and 1970. Davis, building on a good reputation established as a successful schools coach, brought home the only England Grand Slam between 1957 and 1991 when he steered the class of 1980 led by Bill Beaumont to the Five Nations' Holy Grail. But the vintage he had so carefully nurtured prompted his droll comment in 1981 when the Grand Slammers slumped to Five Nations defeats by Wales

and France. Even so, Davis finished his stint as coach in 1982 with only four defeats as England's lead-coach – a near-70 per cent success-rate.

3. This was Will Carling's assessment of New Zealand wing Jonah Lomu's performance after the All Blacks' 45-29 destruction of his England team in the 1995 Rugby World Cup semi-final. The giant New Zealand wing scored four tries, memorably trampling over several England defenders to start the avalanche of points after barely two minutes' play.

4. When South Africa met France in February 1961 at the end of a northern hemisphere tour, the rugby press built their clash up as the match of the century. The Springboks had recently beaten the All Blacks in a home series and completed the Grand Slam of the Home Unions earlier on their tour. France, meanwhile, were the reigning Five Nations champions, unbeaten in the Championship for three years and with a series win in South Africa in 1958 to their credit, as well as a victory over New Zealand in their most recent clash with the All Blacks. The match started with the mother of all fights, with fists and feet flailing everywhere as two giant packs released weeks of pent-up emotions. At length, power lay with the calm control of the smallest man on the pitch: the blazered referee from Gowerton, Gwynne Walters. The little Welshman blew his whistle to draw the two captains together and issued his blunt warning. It worked. The rest of the match was played at a ferocious pace but in the best of spirits, and the result, arguably, was probably the best outcome for the game ended as a scoreless draw.

5. Barry John's instruction to Gareth Edwards when the Welsh half-backs first met for an informal practice near Carmarthen in January 1967. They had just been named to play together for the Probables in the final Welsh trial ahead of that year's Five Nations. The laid-back John quickly tired of his enthusiastic young partner's keenness on a wet Sunday

morning, and eventually turned to Edwards and uttered these famous words. It would be a year, however, before the partnership was consummated for Wales. Barry John gashed his knee and left the field after only three minutes of the trial, delaying their first international outing together until the following season.

6. Irish line-out jumper Bill Mulcahy's instant response when asked by his thrower how he wanted the ball delivered from touch.

7. England skipper Steve Smith delivered the verdict on Colin Smart's medical condition after the prop had mistakenly necked a bottle of aftershave in a drinking game with French adversaries at the France-England post-match dinner in 1982. Smart later summed up the occasion saying, 'About par for a rugby dinner ... from what I can remember.'

8. No set of rugby quotations would be complete without a reference to Sir Tony O'Reilly, wit, businessman and outstanding British & Irish Lion of the 1950s, who once offered this description for the state of the game in his beloved Ireland.

9. Bill Beaumont's alleged under-the-breath response after a Welsh fan had greeted him with a cheerful 'May the best team win' on the eve of England's 1979 game in Cardiff. Wales hadn't lost a Five Nations match at home since 1968 and England hadn't won there since 1963. Beaumont's team were smashed 27-3.

10. Vivid description of Wales flanker Clem Thomas by his old rival Peter Robbins, an Oxford and England flanker. The pair, who played against one another in three successive Wales-England internationals of the late 1950s, later became respected rugby writers and close friends, both with a wicked sense of humour.

POLITICAL CONNECTIONS

1. The well-known rugby referee was that man of many parts, Denis Thatcher. He regularly officiated on the London club scene and enjoyed 80 minutes in the international rugby limelight in April 1956 when he was nominated by the RFU as their touch judge for the France-England match at the old Stade Colombes ground on the Paris outskirts.

2. Derek Wyatt, who won a cap as a replacement for David Duckham against Scotland at Murrayfield in 1976, was the Labour Member of Parliament for Sittingbourne and Sheppey from 1997 until he retired at the 2010 General Election.

3. Dick Spring was the distinguished Irish politician. He won three caps for his country in 1979 when he was playing for the Lansdowne club and entered Irish politics as the Teachta Dála for Kerry North two years later.

4. Clem Thomas was a member of the Liberal Party who stood for Gower at the February 1974 election and was their candidate in Carmarthen in 1979. He also contested the Dyfed seat at the 1978 election for the European Parliament. Despite fighting lively campaigns, he was never elected.

5. Carwyn James, former Welsh rugby international, Welsh language teacher and Llanelli RFC coach, stood for Plaid at the 1970 election. But the man who would steer the Lions to an historic winning series in New Zealand a year later could make little headway in a strongly Labour constituency,

though he did manage to garner sufficient votes to save his deposit. A fervent Nationalist, he polled around 9,000 votes – 'the average Stradey Park gate when the Scarlets were at home,' he later remarked.

6. The French international-turned-Prime Minister was Jacques Chaban Delmas, a French Resistance underground hero who played on the wing in France's first post-war cap match. A Gaullist politician, he first made his mark in peacetime public life when, aged 32, he was elected mayor of Bordeaux in 1947.

7. The three members of that outstanding New Zealand side who sat in the Wellington Parliament were wing Tony Steel, three-quarter Grahame Thorne and half-back Chris Laidlaw. Remarkably, they all served at the same time in 1992–93.

8. Dawie de Villiers played in 25 Tests for South Africa, captaining the Springboks 22 times. After entering the church, he lectured at the Rand Afrikaans University, where he was persuaded to become politically active. He was a member of the South African House of Assembly during the 1970s and served briefly as South Africa's ambassador in London, but returned to his homeland in 1980 to hold a cabinet post with responsibility for trade and industry.

9. Arguably England's most celebrated rugby player until the 1950s was Wavell Wakefield – the one and only 'Wakers', who appeared 31 times in the English scrum between 1920 and 1926 and held the national cap record until 'Budge' Rogers overhauled him in the late 1960s. In 1923, he was the first to demand that England's forwards adopt specialist roles as props, hooker, locks and back row at scrums. Before then, the custom for forwards arriving at scrums was to pack first-up, first-down. He was Swindon's MP from 1935 to 1945 and then sat in the House as the member for St Marylebone, London, until 1963.

10. Trevor Ringland played 31 times for Ireland from 1981–88 as an inventive wing with a deceptive change of pace. An Ulster solicitor, he stood for East Belfast at the 2010 General Election before serving as co-chair of the Northern Ireland Conservatives in 2013–14. He was as formidable a politician as he had been a winger.

BUSINESS MATTERS

1. During his active playing career Tony O'Reilly became managing director of the Heinz Corporation's UK operation, whose most famous advertising campaign of the 1960s and '70s was 'Beanz Meanz Heinz'. He was an automatic choice for Ireland from 1955 until 1963, when business commitments finally restricted his participation in the game to social rugby with London Irish. In 1970, however, he was dramatically recalled for Ireland's game against England at Twickenham when Bill Brown, the chosen wing, dropped out of the starting XV. The former Lion gave the press a field day in their match previews after he arrived for a team practice in a chauffeur-driven Rolls-Royce. He had little to do during the match itself, but was the target for a shoeing when trapped in a ruck during loose play, prompting one wag in the crowd to shout: 'And give his bloody chauffeur a kick while you're at it.' But arguably the best reflection on his recall was from a newspaperman who headed a comment piece 'Heinz Meanz has-Beanz'.

2. The Scottish wing Bill Gammell, who scored twice on his Test debut against Ireland at Murrayfield in 1977 and won five caps before injury forced him to retire from active rugby in 1978, is the oil tycoon who founded Cairn Energy. He has been named UK Entrepreneur of the Year and in 2006 was created Knight Bachelor for services to industry in Scotland.

3. Frank Jacob Slazenger Moss was capped three times in the England packs of 1885 and 1886 before leaving his native

Manchester and settling in New York, where he founded a rugby club, changed his name to Frank Legh (after the Salford street where he had lived as a youngster) Slazenger and set up and ran the American arm of the company founded by his elder brothers.

4. John Eric Greenwood was a director of high street chain Boots. A forward in his playing days, he was one of the small band of internationals capped by England both before and after the First World War. In his long and successful business career he worked closely with Sir Jesse Boot over the sale of the family's famous business empire to the American market, and its subsequent return to British control.

5. Cotton Traders is the well-known leisurewear company founded and run by prop Fran Cotton with his fellow Loughborough Colleges, Sale and England colleague, Steve Smith. Both former England captains, they joined forces off the field to launch the company in 1987.

6. Mike Burton was the bubbly boy they couldn't keep down, whether on the rugby field or pitching for business in the world of sports hospitality and travel. The first man sent off playing for England – against Australia at Brisbane in 1975 – he built an impressive business empire after his playing days were over. He also believed in putting something back into the game, later becoming a backbone of the Barbarian Football Club and bringing his business acumen to the voluntary role of governor at Hartpury College in the Cotswolds, the learning establishment linked with Gloucester's Rugby Academy.

7. The only classic Wallaby who made both the 1947 and 1957 Northern tours was Nick, later Sir Nicholas, Shehadie. A powerfully built tight forward, equally at home at prop or second row, he won 30 caps for Australia before putting plenty of his energy back into the game as an administrator

for the Australian Rugby Union. His services to Sydney business and civic affairs were crowned by two terms as mayor of the city.

8. Self-confessed rugby nut Nigel Wray, who read economics at Bristol University before starting his career in business as a graduate trainee with merchant bankers Singer & Friedlander, was a north London boy educated at Mill Hill School. He was a stalwart of the Old Millhillians RFC for the best part of 30 years, during which time he represented Hampshire as a wing in the County Championship.

9. Bill Beaumont led the North to a famous win against the All Blacks in 1979 and went on the same season to skipper England's first Grand Slam win for 23 years. Forced to retire prematurely on medical grounds in 1982, he made a media name for himself as a TV pundit and resident captain for the BBC quiz show *A Question of Sport*, while at the same time running the family's soft furnishings business from its base in Chorley. He was elected Chairman of World Rugby, formerly the International Board, in May 2016, and received a knighthood in the 2019 New Year Honours List.

10. Sir Wilson Whineray and David Kirk were the victorious New Zealand captains who carried on winning as business leaders. Whineray was in charge of the All Blacks between 1958 and 1965 before reaching the pinnacle of his business career as chairman of Carter Holt, one of the country's leading companies. David Kirk wore the captain's armband when they won the inaugural Rugby World Cup in 1987. He became the CEO of the Fairfax Group from 2005 to 2008 and now holds a number of directorships. He has also chaired the boards of various New Zealand and Australian-based companies.

HALL OF FARMERS

1. John Pullin, who farmed at Aust in the shadows of the original Severn Bridge, took up the England captaincy reins against the Springboks at Johannesburg in June 1972 and opened his account with a memorable 18-9 victory. He followed that with another remarkable away win just over a year later, when England defeated the All Blacks 16-10 in Auckland and completed the rare treble over the Tri-Nations when he led his country to a 20-3 rout of Australia in November 1973.

2. That rustic Welsh front row ran their farming businesses on the fertile slopes of North Pembrokeshire's Preseli Hills. Williams was a sheep farmer near Clynderwen, barely a sheep dip or two away from where his relative Kevin Phillips operated, while John Davies, the youngest of the trio, farmed at Boncath. All three acquired an early taste for rugby while pupils at Ysgol y Preseli in Crymych.

3. At 5ft 4in (1m 62cm) John Abbott King remains the smallest forward capped by England. He farmed on Ben Rhydding (Ilkley) and was a fixture in the England pack between 1911 and 1913, when he was ever-present in the XV that secured England's first Grand Slam. Army Regulations in 1914 stipulated that recruits had to be at least 5ft 6in (1m 68cm), but Jack was resolute when faced with the likelihood of rejection, blagging his way into the King's Army on 12 August 1914 – eight days after war was declared. He was reported missing presumed killed in action at Guillemont two years later.

4. David Rollo was the highly respected Scottish farmer who conditioned himself for rugby through his rigorous farming schedule. The Howe of Fife local hero won 40 caps between 1959 and 1968, matching the then Scotland appearance record established by Hughie McLeod, and toured South Africa with the British & Irish Lions in 1962.

5. The one and only Colin Meads. The uncompromising All Black won 55 caps between 1955 and 1971, a Himalayan career in the days when rugby was an amateur sport, all the while tending to the unrelenting demands of milking, clearing land and shearing sheep on his Te Kuiti farm in New Zealand's King Country.

6. P.J. (Philip) Nel, a farmer from the Kranskop District of KwaZulu-Natal province, skippered the Springboks to a 2-1 series win against the All Blacks in New Zealand. The first two series between the southern hemisphere's premier rugby nations, in 1921 and 1928, had been drawn. Nel's side was hailed as the greatest team to visit New Zealand, but curiously he left himself out for the first Test, which was won by New Zealand. He returned to lead the team to wins in the last two matches of the rubber.

7. Williams was referring to Graham Mourie, the farmer from Taranaki whose calm, firm leadership saw New Zealand through 19 Tests between 1977 and 1981, including the four in Britain and Ireland in 1978 when the All Blacks pulled off their first Grand Slam of the Home Unions. Mourie displayed the charm and intelligence of a diplomat off the field and, possessed of an unwavering moral compass, chose to stand down from selection against South Africa in 1981 on conscientious grounds.

8. The Scottish farmer was the rangy flanker Douglas Elliot, whose back-row plans entrapped the Welsh in those two Murrayfield successes, Scotland winning 6-5 in 1949 and by

a whopping 19-0 two years later against a Welsh side packed with Lions returning from a tour of New Zealand. That was a trip for which Elliot himself would have been a cert, but he declared his unavailability, citing his farming commitments at home as the reason. Away from the fields of play he was a successful sheep breeder renowned for his North Country Cheviots that won prizes at Royal Highland Shows.

9. The Kelso farmer John Jeffrey was the disrupter-in-chief when Scotland sent Will Carling's glory-seekers home to think again. The blond flanker who won 40 caps for his country managed to infiltrate the opposition pack time and again, wrecking England's power game at its very heart and preventing them from exerting any tactical control.

10. Ricky Bartlett of Harlequins was the stand-off whose tactical nous behind a dominant pack was a key factor in England's 1957 Grand Slam season. He took up pig farming in 1955.

AUTHOR! AUTHOR!

1. *Rugger* – now there's a word one rarely hears these days. Long associated with English public school lingo, it remained in common usage until the 1960s but is virtually extinct today. Even so, they didn't come more down-to-earth in the 1950s than the author in question here. Lewis Jones was a typical Welsh lad from Lime Street in the little village of Gorseinon near Swansea before conquering the rugby world at both codes – union for the Royal Navy, Llanelli, Wales and the Lions; league for Leeds and Great Britain.

2. *Code Breaker* was the life story of Jonathan Davies, arguably the most successful dual-code exponent of all time who in 1995, soon after the International Board's relaxation of its amateur ethos, was the first to break the old barriers by returning from league and regaining his place in the Welsh national XV. Today he is a sought-after broadcaster whose incisive summaries and tactical insights reveal his rare depth of knowledge of both codes.

3. Not Mike Catt – as you might have expected from the title – but scrum-half Matt Dawson, who established himself as a pivotal figure in the plans of Sir Clive Woodward during the build-up to and winning of the 2003 Rugby World Cup.

4. The feline metaphor does refer to Mike Catt this time, though given the length of his career and the number of setbacks he overcame you do wonder if *Nine Lives* would have been his preference had Dawson not beaten him to the title. The South African who played for the Eastern Province made

his England debut in 1994, went on to gain 75 caps for his adopted country including appearances in two Rugby World Cup Finals, and retired in 2007 at the age of 36.

5. *Top Cat* was the title of Clive Rowlands's autobiography. It was the nickname his teammates gave him when he was captain of Wales for all 14 of his Test appearances between 1963 and 1965. Democracy or consultation weren't part of the Rowlands approach: he ruled his sides with an iron fist … and they just loved him, calling him after the autocratic alley-cat character in the popular Saturday tea-time comedy cartoon of the time. He went on to serve as coach, selector, team manager and President of the Union in a lifetime devoted to Welsh rugby.

6. Brian Moore was the heartbeat of the England sides of the early 1990s, the man who wore his national pride on his sleeve, stirred his fellow forwards and goaded opponents. His uncompromising style of play earned him the nickname 'Pitbull', the breed which inspired the title of his second autobiography. His first effort, *Brian Moore*, written with the collaboration of the excellent Stephen Jones, rugby correspondent of *The Sunday Times*, had appeared straight after his retirement as a player in 1995. But that sanitised version of his life was written, he said, against the emotional background of an impending divorce. In the update, entirely in his own words, he aimed to capture his personality by taking a longer perspective on his life and rugby career. The result was a riveting read.

7. There's a lot to be said for players putting their life story in print 20 or so years after their active participation in rugby has ended. The Scottish internationalist who took the long view was Jim Renwick. The fabled Hawick centre of excellence waited 22 years before collaborating on a book about the long stay that brought him 52 caps between 1972 and 1984.

8. Hennie Muller was a No. 8 – or eighthman as they call the position in South Africa. Muller, the only Springbok to play in every Test for his country between 1949 and 1953, made the position his own and through careful thought devised the tactical blueprint for the position that is adhered to this day. He was truly the father of the modern position.

9. *The Boot*, published in 1966, chronicled the playing career of Don Clarke who accumulated a then world record 207 points in his 31 Tests between 1956 and 1964 – more than half of the points scored by the New Zealand teams in which he appeared. Moreover, many of his points came from last-minute match-winning scores.

10. The 'Rainbow Warrior' was Francois Pienaar, who projected a polished public image as the captain of the Rainbow Nation when South Africa staged and won the 1995 Rugby World Cup.

FAMILY TIES

1. James McClure (capped by Scotland against England in 1872) and his brother George (capped in the corresponding match of 1873) were the first pair of twins to play Test rugby. Records show that the boys were born on 8 July 1851. Fewer than 20 pairs of twins have won international rugby recognition to date.

2. Jordie, Beauden and Scott Barrett were the fourth trio of brothers to play for the All Blacks after their contemporaries the Whitelocks, and the Nicholls and Brownlies in the 1920s. Their unique position in New Zealand rugby, however, is that they are the only three brothers to appear together in a run-on Test XV, playing in the 38-18 win against France at Auckland in 2018. Previously, the three were on the field at different times against Samoa in 2017, and were briefly together through substitutions against the Lions in Auckland later the same season.

3. The McLeans and Murphys share the distinction of providing the only male lines of a grandfather, father and son capped at rugby union in the English-speaking world. The McLean family included six Test players. Doug, who played three internationals against the British/Irish team in 1904, had three rugby-playing sons who became Wallabies: Doug junior (1933–36), Bill (1946–47) and Jack (uncapped but toured New Zealand in 1946). Bill's son, Peter, was a strapping forward who played in 15 Tests for Australia between 1978 and 1982. Two more grandsons of Doug senior, Paul and Jeff, also played Test rugby for Australia in

the 1970s and 1980s. The unique Irish family comprised Noel senior (capped between 1930 and 1933), his son Noel junior (1958–69) and grandson Kenny, who was capped between 1990 and 1992.

4. The Old family from Yorkshire would have had their sporting loyalties to the brothers Alan and Chris split twice on Saturdays in February 1974. While Alan played fly-half for England against Scotland at Murrayfield and Ireland at Twickenham, younger sibling Chris was in the England XI as a bowler for Tests against the West Indies in Port of Spain and Kingston.

5. The Test careers of Jim and Finlay Calder never overlapped. Jim won 27 caps for Scotland (1981–85) and toured New Zealand with the 1983 Lions before giving way in the national team's back row to his twin, Finlay, for 34 matches from 1986–91. Finlay skippered the Lions to a series win in Australia in 1989.

6. Tana Umaga lined up on the wing for New Zealand against his brother, Mike, at full-back for Samoa in a Test match at Albany's North Harbour Stadium in June 1999.

7. The 2017 Ireland-England match broke new ground because a coach was on the opposite side to his son. Andy Farrell was a member of the Irish coaching staff and his son, Owen, was England's outside-half.

8. Salesi and Campese Ma'afu were the first pair of brothers who made their Test debuts on opposite sides in the same match and uniquely went head-to-head at scrum time. Salesi was the Wallabies' tight-head and his brother occupied the loose-head for Fiji.

9. There were three pairs of brothers in the Irish XV at Cardiff in 1924. George and Harry Stephenson formed one half of

the three-quarter line, Tom Hewitt played on the wing with his 17-year-old brother Frank operating at outside-half, and the veteran Collopy brothers, Dick and Billy, were in the pack. To complete the extensive family rugby ties in that Irish XV, Jim McVicker had two brothers who were Irish caps in the 1920s, and both Bob Collis and Charles Hallaran's fathers had played against Wales 40 years earlier.

10. And who wouldn't be proud to say that he was capped by his country? But the real twist to Feidlim McLoughlin's proud boast was that his famous brother Ray won 40 of those 41 caps! Feidlim's only appearance for Ireland was against Australia in 1976.

IN THE LINE OF FIRE

1. These are the only four rugby international players who were awarded the Victoria Cross (VC). Johnston and Crean were decorated for their bravery in the Second Boer War; Harvey and Harrison won their medals for courage shown in the First World War.

2. Noel Chavasse was the only person to win the VC twice in the First World War. He qualified as a doctor after studying at Trinity College, Oxford, and joined the Royal Army Medical Corps (RAMC) in 1913. He was awarded the Military Cross (MC) for gallantry at Hooge in 1915 and was decorated with the highest honour for bravery at the Battle of Guillemont (1916) and then again at Passchendaele in 1917, where he subsequently died of wounds sustained while tending injured soldiers.

3. Charles Upham, another like Chavasse who had 'played the game', became the only soldier to receive the VC twice in the Second World War. The New Zealander was decorated for conspicuous bravery in Crete (1941) and in Egypt a year later. Upham is the only combat soldier among the three men who have won the VC and bar in Commonwealth military history.

4. Ronnie Poulton and Freddie Turner were two of the 11 war casualties who had played in the 1914 Calcutta Cup thriller at Inverleith, a match which England eventually won by 16-15 to seal the Triple Crown. The two former captains were playing members of the Liverpool club in 1914. Poulton,

who died at Ploegsteert Wood in 1915, had changed his name to Poulton-Palmer in 1914 after receiving a legacy from his grandfather George Palmer, a founder of the Huntley & Palmer biscuit company. Freddie Turner predeceased him by barely four months, killed in action near Kemmel in northern France.

5.   Edgar Mobbs, who won seven England caps between 1909 and 1910, raised a force of more than 200 soldiers to enlist in the Northamptonshire Regiment, a company that became known as 'Mobbs's Own'. He was a noted member of the Barbarians and led the side in their charity match against Wales at Cardiff in 1915. The first annual Mobbs Memorial match between the East Midlands and the Barbarians took place in February 1921.

6.   Swannell was a member of the 1899 Lions to Australia (playing three Tests) and returned there with Bedell-Sivright's Lions of 1904 (featuring in all four Tests), before settling in Sydney, New South Wales, and winning Australian Test honours against New Zealand in 1905. A Major in the Australian Imperial Force, he was one of two capped rugby players killed in action at the start of the Gallipoli offensive on 25 April 1915, subsequently known as Anzac Day. Teddy Larkin, a journalist who became a state MP and was secretary of the fledgling NSW Rugby League after winning a Union cap for Australia against New Zealand in 1903, was the other Anzac Day casualty. It should be remembered, however, that nearly a dozen other rugby internationals lost their lives during or as the result of the Gallipoli action.

7.   Maurice Turnbull, who was caught in machine-gun fire and killed in action near the Normandy village of Montchamp in 1944, is the only dual international capped by Wales at rugby union (against England and Ireland in 1933) and England at cricket (nine Tests, 1930–36). A fine all-round sportsman, he also played hockey for Wales in 1929.

8. The Ireland and 1938 Lions lock Blair 'Paddy' Mayne was an original member of the Special Air Service (SAS) who won the DSO and three bars for his selfless bravery in the North African, Mediterranean and European theatres of war. That his extraordinary courage was never rewarded with the VC is one of the mysteries surrounding this larger-than-life Ulsterman.

9. Okey Geffin was captured at Tobruk during the Western Desert Campaign and spent the latter part of the Second World War in a prisoner-of-war camp at Thorn in Poland. There, he found a stray rugby ball and dedicated the long hours of captivity to practising place-kicking. He was raised barely a touch-kick from Johannesburg's famous Ellis Park ground and as a child idolised Gerry Brand, the Springbok whose siege-gun kicking and unerring accuracy had put Wallabies, All Blacks and Lions to the sword during the 1930s. Geffin set about emulating the maestro, with the result that when Springbok Tests resumed against New Zealand in 1949, he was an automatic choice for the 'Boks as a place-kicking prop. He stepped onto the pages of rugby history in the series-opener at Newlands, landing five penalties with a stunning display of the kicking art. His points reversed an 11-3 half-time deficit and converted it to a 15-11 triumph that elevated him to national hero status.

10. John MacCallum was a son of the manse. His father was a Church of Scotland minister who preached that war and anything remotely connected with war was sinful. John was a medical doctor who inherited his father's strong faith and became rugby's best-known conscientious objector in the First World War. He took such a strong moral stance to the war that he even declined an offer of service exemption in exchange for treating wounded soldiers returning home from the Western Front. As a result, he was imprisoned and sentenced to hard labour on a manure farm near Edinburgh.

STAGE AND SCREEN

1. Eric Liddell was the noted Scottish rugby internationalist who won seven caps on the wing in 1922 and 1923 before giving up the sport to concentrate on his athletic preparations for the 1924 Summer Olympics. He and Harold Abrahams were contenders for gold in the 100m sprint, but Liddell's Christian beliefs compelled him to withdraw from the event at the Paris Games because the heats were scheduled for a Sunday. That cleared the field for Abrahams to claim his medal, but administrative moves behind the scenes enabled Liddell to switch events and win gold in the 400m.

2. *Alive,* starring Ethan Hawke, is the gripping tale of the desperate fight for survival by the rugby team from the Old Christians RFC in Montevideo after their charter plane crash-landed in the Andes during a flight to Santiago to play a match in Chile.

3. Richard Todd, who starred as Guy Gibson in the 1955 film *The Dam Busters* and as Lt-Col. John Wynter in *D-Day the Sixth of June* (1956), was of Anglo-Irish stock. His father, Andrew William Palethorpe Todd, was Ireland's last line of defence in three Five Nations internationals in the two seasons before the First World War. Todd senior, like many of the pre-war Irish caps, was a medical doctor. He served with the Royal Army Medical Corps and was awarded the Military Cross during the Great War.

4. The red-haired Ireland and Lions wing Tony O'Reilly was the darling of the crowds who flocked to see the 1955 Lions on

tour in South Africa, and his looks attracted close attention from film moguls who considered him for the lead in their production of *Ben-Hur*. The film eventually hit the cinema screens in 1959 with Charlton Heston as the fall-back choice in the role for which the virile Irishman was ideally suited.

5. Roy Kinnear senior, who was a British & Irish Lion in South Africa in 1924 and played three times for Scotland in 1926, was the father of Roy Kinnear and grandfather of Rory Kinnear, both of whom have long lists of television, radio, stage and film credits to their names.

6. New Zealand had been playing in Ireland since 1905 before suffering their first defeat on Irish soil in October 1978. John Breen's play celebrated the occasion, recreating the wonderful atmosphere surrounding the day Graham Mourie's All Blacks were Munstered 12-0 at Limerick's Thomond Park. The Munster side coached by Tom Kiernan scored their points through Christy Cantillon, who crossed after Jimmy Bowen's electrifying first-half run down the left wing. Tony Ward converted and landed two dropped goals in the second half. The play was first staged at Waterpark RFC in the West of Ireland in 1999, was a West End hit in 2002 and was later a box-office success in Australia.

7. *Invictus* was the film telling the story of how South Africa's post-apartheid President Nelson Mandela (Morgan Freeman) and Springbok rugby skipper Francois Pienaar (Matt Damon) used the 1995 Rugby World Cup to unite their country into the Rainbow Nation and motivate the team to win the sport's most prestigious event.

8. All-round good egg and man of many parts Martin Bayfield is the former international who has been a regular in the *Harry Potter* series,

and his other screen credits include the BBC programmes *Crimewatch* and *Celebrity MasterChef.* He won 31 caps for England between 1991 and 1996 and was a Lion in 1993, appearing in all three Tests of the series against New Zealand. In addition, he is an accomplished after-dinner speaker and presents and reports on Premiership rugby on British television.

9. *Friends: The One With All The Rugby* was an episode first aired in 1998. To impress Emily, his British girlfriend, Ross takes up the challenge made by a group of her friends visiting from home to play rugby. Mark Thomas, the son of the former Welsh rugby captain Clem Thomas, was cast as one of the British visitors.

10. The television film was *Grand Slam*, starring Windsor Davies and Hugh Griffith. Set over the weekend of the 1977 France-Wales match which decided that season's title, it followed the adventures of a group of Welsh supporters let loose in Paris and included footage of the match and players. It was first aired on the eve of the Grand Slam decider between the same two teams at Cardiff in March of the following year.

FAMOUS FIRSTS
AND LASTS

1. Billy Bancroft kicked Test rugby's first penalty goal. With England leading 11-9 at Cardiff in 1893, Bancroft stepped forward to land the points that won the match for Wales and set them on the path to their first Triple Crown.

2. M.J.K. Smith was the last of the small band of dual internationals capped by England at rugby and cricket. He played stand-off for England against Wales at Twickenham in 1956 and appeared in 50 cricket Tests between 1958 and 1972, many as captain.

3. In 2007, England played at Croke Park, the hallowed home of Ireland's Gaelic sports community (GAA), for the first time. The ground staged several major rugby union events while Lansdowne Road underwent refurbishment. Brian O'Driscoll led the first Ireland rugby team to face England on a ground whose cultural significance resonates with the Irish diaspora worldwide.

4. Jerry Shea was the first international player to run through the card of scoring actions in a Test. His full house of a try, a conversion, a penalty and two dropped goals in a 16-point personal haul helped his country to a 19-5 win. You'd have expected him to win hero status for such a performance, but instead he was severely criticised for perceived selfishness, and after unsuccessfully trying to reprise the feat against Scotland in the next match, he was dropped from the side.

5. Donna Kennedy, the Scottish Women's No. 8 from Biggar, was the first internationalist – male or female – to notch up a century of appearances for Scotland and the first woman to play in 100 Tests for any nation. A member of Scotland Women's 1998 Grand Slam side, she finished her career with 115 caps and was for many years women's rugby's most-capped player.

6. Harry Frazer was credited with the first penalty try recorded in any Test. During the Brisbane international on the 1947 All Blacks tour of Australia, a Wallaby obstructed him in the act of scoring and the referee, Tom Moore, had no hesitation in awarding a penalty try.

7. The Wales-England game at Wembley on Sunday 11 April 1999 was the last ever staged in the long-running Five Nations tournament and the distinction of scoring its last try went to Scott Gibbs. He beat five would-be tacklers to score, with Neil Jenkins's subsequent conversion bringing Wales an unexpected 32-31 victory. The next season Italy were admitted to the European elite and the competition became the Six Nations.

8. Maggi Alphonsi broke the male domination of this prestigious rugby award in 2010, polling more votes among rugby writers than New Zealand captain Richie McCaw. The Saracens and England Women's flanker won 74 international caps, was made an MBE and was inducted to the World Rugby Hall of Fame in 2016.

9. Wallace and Clarke bookended the handful of goals from marks that New Zealand kicked in their Test history. The scoring device ceased to exist in the late 1970s when the free-kick clause entered rugby's laws. Wallace's feat of landing two goals from marks in one match was unique in Test history and occurred in New Zealand's first official international, in 1903. Don Clarke's prodigious effort against England at

Lancaster Park in 1963 was a match-winner from his own half, a goal that the local newspaper described as 'The Daddy of All Kicks'.

10. Brothers had appeared in Test rugby since the birth of the international game in the 1870s, and some had even played Tests together long before the renowned Browns arrived on the scene. But before 1970, there had never been an instance of one brother replacing another during the course of a Test. At Cardiff in 1970, Peter Brown went off nursing a badly pulled calf muscle early in the second half and his brother, Gordon, came on as substitute to complete this familial first.

BLOOPERS

1. Clive Woodward was a gifted centre in England's 1980 Grand Slam, but it was his moment of madness playing as a wing that cost the Lions dearly in Port Elizabeth. Ten minutes from time in a match they needed to win to keep the series alive, the Lions were leading 10-6 when Springbok fly-half Naas Botha nudged the ball into the Lions 25 on Woodward's side of the field. Instead of picking it up and kicking for the safety of touch 30 yards upfield, Woodward nonchalantly side-footed the ball into touch from where he was standing, then compounded his carelessness by turning his back and retiring to his goal line to prepare for the ensuing line-out. Springboks Gerrie Germishuys and Theuns Stofberg were quick to realise the golden opportunity that was now presented and quickly took the throw-in before the Lions could re-group, and from an exchange of quick passes Germishuys scored the try which Botha converted from near touch to win the match, and with it the series for South Africa.

2. The French wing crossed the line but delayed touching down in an effort to score nearer the posts. Meanwhile England's Richard Harding dashed across and dislodged the ball from Estève's grasp, saving the day for his team to escape from the match with a 9-all draw.

3. The Wizard of Oz, David Campese, was famed for the bold approach he brought to rugby in his playing day. At Sydney in 1989, however, his wild pass to his full-back near the Australian goalline was gobbled up by that hungry scavenger

Ieuan Evans for the shock try that turned the game into a 19-18 Lions win that sealed the series for the tourists.

4. Late in the game Bath were trailing 20-22 when Freddie Burns crossed near the posts and was blowing a celebratory kiss to supporters when the Toulouse wing, Maxime Médard, dashed across to flip the ball out of the showboating full-back's hands. Burns was replaced immediately but in the few remaining minutes of the match Bath were unable to score.

5. Bristol's Mike Titcomb, one of the best British referees of the 1960s and early '70s, was badly tricked by parallax and the celebratory gamesmanship of several Welsh players into awarding Gareth Edwards an equalising dropped goal that clearly missed the posts. He was probably the only person among the 50,000 or so present who believed the goal was good. The crowd were incensed and the usually good-natured Irish supporters rushed the pitch, causing a long delay. Fortunately the Irish players accepted the decision with good grace superficially, which helped calm the crowd, but privately they must have been seething at the referee's honest mistake. At length justice was seen to be done. In the tenth minute of added time flanker Mick Doyle went over for the try that broke the deadlock, Ireland winning 9-6, but it was a day that Mike Titcomb, who needed a police escort after the final whistle, never forgot.

6. Terry Davies was heavily criticised for electing to face a gale-force wind and driving rain in the first half after winning the toss. The upshot was that his forwards were a spent force by half-time, having defended bravely against a juggernaut Springbok pack. South Africa, who won 3-0, had exploited the elements early on to score the decisive points with a penalty downwind and from in front of the posts before the ball had become a sodden, muddy mass that was too heavy to kick and impossible to handle.

7. Leading 31-25 late in the match, Lawrence Dallaglio's side were awarded a penalty in a kickable position. A successful shot would have given them an impregnable 9-point cushion, but instead of asking Jonny Wilkinson to go for the posts the popular English skipper opted for a kick into the corner. The Welsh exit strategy was perfectly executed and eventually play reached English territory, where Scott Gibbs embarked on a clattering run that culminated in a try that Neil Jenkins converted for a totally unpredictable 32-31 victory. As a result England were denied the Grand Slam, and the last title in Five Nations history was gifted to Scotland, who had beaten France in Paris the day before.

8. Chris Robshaw had to plead guilty to a similar offence to Lawrence Dallagio's when he shunned a 78th-minute chance to give Owen Farrell a penalty kick at goal that would have drawn England's key 2015 Rugby World Cup pool match with Wales at Twickenham. The captain directed his kicker to aim for the corner, hoping that the winning try would follow from the subsequent line-out. The Welsh held out to win, and England's defeat by Australia a week later sent them tumbling out of their own World Cup before the pool stage was complete.

9. On a windswept Murrayfield Andy Irvine with Ian McLauchlan's steadying hand on the ball whacked it high and true through the posts from a penalty near halfway. So, 6-0 to Scotland thought the Scottish team and 55,000 of their ecstatic spectators, but to their consternation Mr Pattinson disallowed the kick, ruling that as McLauchlan was in front of the ball he was offside. He was wrong. A player holding the ball for a place kick does not have to be behind it. It was a howler that cost Mr Pattinson his Test career, for although he apologised to the Scots after the match, he was never again invited to control an international.

10. England were leading 19-18 with the match approaching injury time when Wales were awarded a scrum. It was (once again) Clive Woodward's temporary lack of concentration that proved costly when he drifted offside in front of his posts inside his own 22 and Steve Fenwick kicked Wales to a 21-19 win. Still, every cloud has its silver lining, and mistakes often provide the best learning opportunities. When he became head coach of the England side, the TCUP mantra he drilled into his players – Think Carefully Under Pressure – underpinned the success of the 2003 Rugby World Cup-winning side.

RUG-LIT

1. Thomas Hughes's *Tom Brown's Schooldays* recreates the Rugby School of the author's youth. William Webb Ellis almost certainly didn't invent the rugby union game, but the position the school holds in the sport's evolution is unchallenged and Hughes's classic describes in a vivid passage how the game was practised there in the 1840s and '50s.

2. Macdonell's much-loved book describes the naïve Scotsman Donald Cameron's search for background about English character in the difficult years between the wars. The rugby passage in the book is a description of his December visit to a foggy Twickenham to enjoy a ploughman's lunch and witness the Oxford-Cambridge Varsity match.

3. Tuppy Glossop features as Bertie Wooster's friend in the P.G. Wodehouse masterpiece *Very Good, Jeeves*. Wodehouse had developed a lifelong love for rugby during his schooldays at Dulwich College and in this story the hapless Glossop reveals an unexpected aspect of his character while turning out for his village in a grudge 'rugby' match that more closely resembles *cnapan*, the lawless street football of the Middle Ages, than the 20th-century game.

4. Not surprisingly, perhaps, this description of a scrum is offered by a hooker, the player at the very heart of every scrum.

5. Michael Bond's loveable Paddington Bear plays for the Peruvians during a return to his old school in the story *Paddington in Touch*.

6. The late Michael Green's trilogy *Art of Coarse Rugby*, *Even Coarser Rugby* and *Rugby Alphabet* sold more than half a million copies, appealing to men and women of all rugby-playing abilities. The books grew from his series of Sunday newspaper articles in which his sharp observations and witty turn of phrase won him a large and devoted following which extended far beyond mere rugby folk.

7. *A Clubbable Woman* is the first in Reginald Hill's Dalziel and Pascoe crime series. The dynamic duo investigates the case of a rugby player's murdered wife and concludes at Twickenham during an international match.

8. The winners of the Ranfurly Shield, a major trophy in New Zealand's domestic game, are kidnapped in Heather Kidd's lively tale and the plot develops with threats to stop a New Zealand tour to South Africa.

9. The novelist John Buchan dedicated *The 39 Steps* to Thomas Nelson and it has been said that the character of Richard Hannay, the chivalrous hero of the spy thriller, was based on the Scottish rugby player. Buchan and Nelson had been contemporaries at Oxford and later worked together in the Nelson family's publishing company. There are strong grounds, too, for believing that Nelson was thinly disguised as 'Morrison', who scores Scotland's corner try during their dramatic comeback to beat the touring Australians in Buchan's novel *Castle Gay*. '[In] one of those sudden gifts of fortune which make Rugby an image of life ... the Scottish left centre, one Morrison, an Academical from Oxford, dodged the Kangaroo full-back with a neat swerve [and] scored in the corner.' Thomas Nelson was killed in action at Arras in 1917.

10. Lloyd Jones's 2008 book recreates the events surrounding the visit made to Britain, Ireland, France and North America by the First All Blacks of 1905 captained by Dave Gallaher.

NEVER MIND
THE WEATHER

1. The 1960 Wales-South Africa Test was played in a monsoon. After an hour of incessant rain the Arms Park had become such a mud bath that the goal lines and touchlines were completely obliterated. Referee Jack Taylor offered to call it a day when he realised how difficult his job was becoming but Terry Davies, the Welsh skipper, insisted the game run its course. Mr Taylor told a local reporter afterwards: 'I cannot remember worse weather conditions in any match I have refereed – it was worse than when I took the Wales-Ireland match here in 1957.' That night the River Taff behind the western end of the ground burst its banks, leaving the Arms Park under 3ft (0.9m) of water.

2. Both sides were issued with thermal underwear when they met at the Arms Park in January 1963 during the Arctic winter that has gone down in British weather annals as the country's coldest since the Second World War. The Welsh XV were even offered mittens, and the national anthems were sung in the players' absence so that they didn't have to stand around shivering in the bitter cold. The ground staff worked miracles to ensure the fixture went ahead and covered the playing surface with 30 tons of straw. However, when that protective layer was removed shortly before the match it was discovered that frost had penetrated the in-goal areas, rendering them so concrete-hard that they had to be shortened for safety reasons.

3. The 1981–82 Wallabies were marooned at their hotel in Penarth in January 1982 after a blanket of snow covered

Britain from coast to coast on the eve of their final tour fixture. The Wallabies were due to fly home two days later so there was no scope for the game to be rearranged, and for the only time in Cardiff's history a big representative match had to be cancelled owing to the weather. The tourists were snowbound for four days and eventually had to be airlifted to London in a fleet of helicopters to catch their flight home.

4.   Driving rain whipped up by an icy south-westerly wind made this the bitterest of days even for the umbrella-and-coat brigade watching at Lansdowne Road. The weather affected Ireland's captain, George Stephenson, so badly that he went off 'staggering and practically in a state of collapse from exposure ... in probably the severest game of rugby ever played', according to one reporter. He was treated for hypothermia after departing with Ireland leading 6-0 with the wind, and his side maintained their dominance despite his second-half absence to hold out for a win.

5.   On 24 January 1925 a partial eclipse of the sun was visible in Britain. The Scottish rugby authorities took the decision to start the match 10 minutes before the scheduled kick-off time so as to avoid the possibility of poor light interfering with play late in the game, as the eclipse reached its maximum. In the event, the afternoon was bright so the later stages of the international were not adversely affected by the movements of the heavenly bodies. One correspondent reporting Scotland's easy 25-4 win emphasised that 'the sun shone brightly until the critical moment [and] the eclipse had nothing to do with the result. Rather it was Scotland, not the solar system, that organised the eclipse.'

6.   The 1908 England-Wales clash, the only Home Nations Championship match ever staged on the ground of Bristol City Football Club, took place in dense fog. Recalling the game many years later, Rhys Gabe, one of the Welsh players who took part in their 28-18 victory, vividly described how

no spectators could be seen from the middle of the pitch, adding: 'We had to rely more on our ears than our eyes to discover where the ball was bouncing.'

7. The wind and rain in Wellington for the 1913 New Zealand-Australia clash was so severe that the referee, taking pity on the players, gave them shorter spells facing the difficult conditions by splitting the match into a game of four 20-minute quarters instead of the usual two halves. The All Blacks won 30-5.

8. The matches in Northern Ireland in 1885 and in the USA in 1991 are the only ones involving Tier One rugby nations that have been abandoned owing to severe weather. In 1885, heavy rain flooded the Ormeau Road ground in Belfast, forcing Hugh Kelly, the referee, to call the match off after barely 30 minutes. Scotland, who were leading by a try to nil at the time, agreed to expunge the result on condition the Irish consented to a replay in Edinburgh a fortnight later. The USA-France game in Colorado in 1991 kicked off in a downpour that quickly developed into a severe electric storm and was abandoned on safety grounds before half-time. The French team were leading 10-3 but as they were scheduled to travel home soon after the match, there was no opportunity to arrange a replay and so the result stood.

9. Instead of playing a match against Wasps, which had been cancelled owing to a frozen ground, the San Isidro team made a beeline for London's Oxford Street where they went shopping for duffel coats. In fact, keeping warm in the Arctic winter of '63 was the toughest challenge of their eight-week tour of England, Scotland, Ireland and France.

10. The dates scheduled for the 1978 and 2012 fixtures coincided with weekends when Paris was gripped by cold snaps that sent the thermometer deep into negative territory and froze grounds across the French capital. Yet on both

occasions teams and spectators were encouraged to travel, and assembled in Paris expecting the matches to be staged. In 1978, the FFR overruled safety concerns voiced by players, Irish officials and even the referee, and decided to stage the game. Luckily the only injuries suffered were cuts, grazes and friction burns, but the cavalier attitude of the French Union in exposing players to danger was later criticised. Although they were not prepared to take the same risks 34 years later when they did postpone the match, they still managed to raise public ire by delaying their decision until barely an hour before kick-off. Long-suffering fans already settled in their Stade de France seats were thus faced with the additional expense of a return trip to Paris three weeks later when the match eventually went ahead.

ABOUT
THE AUTHOR

In a 60-year fascination with the sport, John Griffiths has played, coached, refereed and written about rugby union.

● ●

'In rugby you kick the ball; in association you kick the man if you cannot kick the ball; and in Gaelic you kick the ball if you cannot kick the man.'

Irish scribe Jacques MacCarthy, describing the variations of football played in Ireland in the late 19th century.

● ●